SPITFIRE

THE HISTORY OF A LEGEND

WRITTEN BY MIKE LEPINE

sona
BOOKS

sona BOOKS

© Sona Books Ltd 2020

First Published Sona Books Ltd 2020

WARNING: For private domestic use only, any unauthorised Copying, hiring,
lending or public performance of this book is illegal.

CAT NO: SON0416

Photography courtesy of

Cover Image © under licence from SWA Fine Art Publishers Limited

Getty images:

- Martyn Goddard/Corbis
- Virginia Turbett/Redferns
- Ebet Roberts/Redferns
- Paul Natkin
- Michael Putland
- Richard E. Aaron/Redferns
- The LIFE Picture Collection
- Stuart Mostyn/Redferns

- Brian Rasic
- Peter Still/Redferns
- Mick Hutson/Redferns
- Tim Mosenfelder
- Karl Walter
- Steve Thorne/Redferns
- Martin Philbey/Redferns
- Jazz Archiv Hamburg/ullstein bild

- Francesco Degasperi/AFP
- VCG/VCG
- Francesco Castaldo\Mondadori Portfolio
- Gonzales Photo/Terje Dokken/PYMCA/Avalon/UIG
- J. A. Hampton / Stringer
- Central Press / Stringer
- Imperial War Museums
- Photo 12

All other images Wiki Commons

Book layout & design Darren Grice at Ctrl-d

Copy Editor Tom O'Neill

Made in EU.

ISBN: 978-1-912918-25-6

CONTENTS

'It is said that the Spitfire is too beautiful to be a fighting machine. I sometimes think it's true, but then what better fighter could you want?'

Squadron Leader Neville Duke

'...one of the first things I impressed on my pilots was that you did not 'strap yourself in', you 'buckled the Spitfire on', like girding on armour in days of old...'

Squadron Leader Wilfrid Duncan Smith

'It was a super aircraft, it was absolutely. It was so sensitive on the controls. There was no heaving, or pulling and pushing and kicking. You just breathed on it and when you wanted, if you wanted to turn, you just moved your hands slowly and she went... She really was the perfect flying machine. I've never flown anything sweeter. I've flown jets right up to the Venom, but nothing, nothing like her. Nothing like a Spitfire.'

Flight Sergeant George ' Grumpy' Unwin

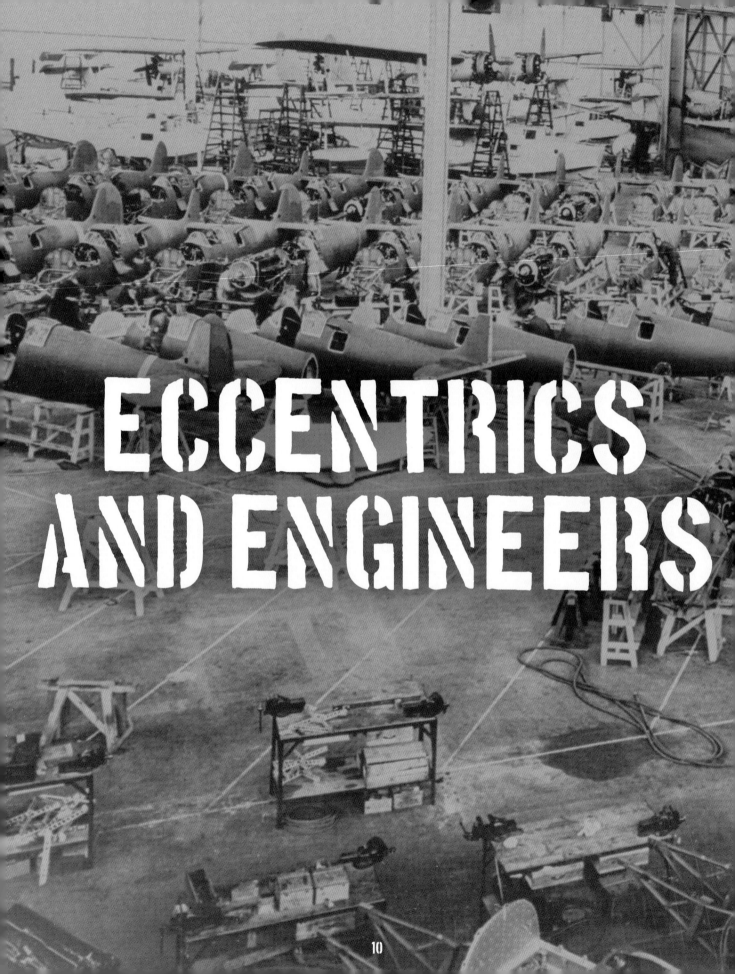

ECCENTRICS AND ENGINEERS

SUPERMARINE

Powered flight was like catnip to Edwardian eccentrics, providing boundless opportunities for japes, hijinks and derring-do. One such eccentric was the Honourable Noel Pemberton Billing, the founder of Supermarine. By turns an adventurer, theatrical impresario and publisher of British South African Autocar magazine (there were no cars in South Africa at the time), Billing had two great obsessions in his life — aviation and lesbianism.

Had Billing endeavoured to combine his twin passions, the future of British aviation might have been very different. As it was, in 1914 he created Pemberton-Billing Ltd on the site of an old coal wharf on the banks of the River Itchen in Southampton and set about designing and building flying boats. His reasoning was that, since the world was comprised mostly of ocean, water would somehow inevitably feature in the future of flight. Billing had already designed three aircraft types, two of which actually got off the ground. In rapid succession now he created the P.B.1 (the Pemberton Billing 1) which was a single-seater seaplane capable of — if not flight — then a sporting frog-like hop into the air and the PB9 single-seater scout . His more bizarre designs included a flying boat that could eject its wings if needed to become a powerful motorboat and the Nighthawk, a rickety quadruplane packing a powerful searchlight and a small artillery piece for Zeppelin hunting. None attracted much support or military interest.

An early devotee of conspiracy theories, Billing became increasingly convinced that Britain was about to be destroyed by a secret society of 47,000 Lesbians and other 'perverts' who were working for the Kaiser to undermine British moral fortitude. They even included Prime Minister Herbert Asquith's wife Margot. Fearing that the British establishment was not taking the promise of aviation or the threat of Lesbianism quite seriously enough, Billing decided to run for parliament. By 1916, he was the elected M.P. for East Hertfordshire. Worried about being accused of a conflict of interest, Billing then handed the ownership of his fledgling aviation company over to his Works Manager Hubert Scott-Paine.

Scott-Paine, colloquially known as 'Ginger' because of his shock of bright red hair, had started his association with Billing as Billing's chauffeur. Before that he had earned a living as a prize-fighter touring fairgrounds up and down the country. Billing — also a keen pugilist — had employed him as a chauffeur primarily for his boxing skills. Whenever the fancy took him, Billing would have Scott-Paine stop the car and the two men would spar by the roadside in the interest of keeping Billing's fighting skills up to par. Despite his odd career path, Scott-Paine was at least grammar school educated and seriously interested in aviation. Whereas Billing was obsessed with water, Scott-Paine loved speed.

✝ Noel Pemberton Billing

✛ Reginald Joseph Mitchell

With Billing gone, he renamed Pemberton-Billing Ltd as the Supermarine Aviation Company.

R.J. MITCHELL

Reginald Joseph Mitchell was born on 20 May 1895 in Kidsgrove, Staffordshire. His father, Herbert Mitchell was a teacher turned Master Printer and dedicated Freemason. The second eldest of five children, Mitchell grew up in the relative comfort and security of Victoria Cottage on the outskirts of Stoke-on-Trent where the grime and smoke of the Potteries could not reach. The family had a maid and spacious gardens to lounge in, as well as outbuildings and stables converted into children's' playrooms.

Right from the earliest age, Mitchell demonstrated a very considerable aptitude for mathematics. Unusually though, his teachers noticed that he was also imaginative and artistic. He was a quiet, shy child with a slight speech impediment that he carried over into adulthood — but this didn't mean that he was at all meek. He inherited his mother's strong stubborn streak and also had a fiery temper and the physical build to back it up.

Mitchell first became interested in aviation when Colonel Sam Cody visited Britain in 1908 to give a flying demonstration. The idea of flight absolutely galvanised Mitchell and his younger brother Eric, and the two children would design and build their own bamboo and paper gliders to be flown out on the lawns. His other hobbies included sports, racing pigeons and inventing things. He designed and built his own billiards table for the siblings to play with, as well as a rudimentary

electric light system to replace the gas lighting in his bedroom.

In 1911, at the age of sixteen, Mitchell left his grammar school and his father secured him an apprenticeship. Mitchell had set his heart on going into aviation, but there were no opportunities locally. Instead he became an apprentice at Kerr, Stuart & Co, a local locomotive engineering firm. It was company policy for every

apprentice to start at the bottom, and Mitchell hated it from the first day. The middle class grammar school boy loathed the idea of travelling into work every day in blue overalls and clutching his thermos and packed lunch, just like the lowest oik. He detested even more coming home each night in dirty overalls covered in grease and soot and oil. Mitchell begged his father to let him leave, but Mitchell senior simply told him he had to go — and like it. Mitchell's temper simmered long and deep…

As a new boy, one of Mitchell's tasks at the firm was to make the foreman his mug of tea. Possibly to wind Mitchell up, the foreman one day spat it out and told him it '*tasted like piss'*. The next day, Mitchell urinated in the kettle and then served the tea up to the foreman as usual. He sipped it, smiled and announced, '*B*loody *good mug of tea, Mitchell! Why can't you make it like this every day?'* History does not record if Mitchell did so from then on.

Somehow, Mitchell made it through his five years at Kerr, Stuart & Co. The anger he felt at being a common engineer lifted when eventually he left the company workshops and was moved upstairs to the drawing office, where he didn't have to wear the dreaded blue overalls and where he was able to mix with an altogether different class of young men. Throughout the five years of his apprenticeship, Mitchell

also attended night school in the hope of bettering his prospects, studying engineering drawing, mechanics and higher mathematics. His abilities won him several prizes during this time.

In 1916, he left Kerr Stuart. He did not want to spend his life there. With World War One raging, he tried to sign up to fight with the RFC twice, but was rejected both times on the grounds that his engineering skills were needed on the Home Front. He tried teaching part time, but that did not particularly appeal. A year passed, and then Mitchell got wind of a job far away in Southampton, as the personal assistant to Hubert Scott-Paine, now Head of Supermarine. The interview went well and he was offered the job by 'Ginger' on the spot. Mitchell never went home. He stayed in Southampton and requested his things be sent down to him.

LIFE AT SUPERMARINE

Supermarine may have been founded and run by eccentrics, but it was a well-functioning company. It could recognise talent, and knew how to put that talent to best use. Mitchell spent a year as assistant to Scott-Paine before being promoted to the post of assistant works

✈ L-R: Supermarine factory, Southampton

✈ The Supermarine Seagull V, an amphibian flying boat is launched by catapult for the first time at the Royal Aircraft Establishment, Farnborough, 27th March 1934

manager. Mitchell took this as a sign that he was now sufficiently established at Supermarine. He briefly returned home to Stoke-on-Trent to marry his long time sweetheart, Florence Dayson, a headmistress over ten years his age, and to bring her back to Southampton. The couple rented a home, joined the local tennis club to mingle with Southampton's great and good and Mitchell bought a motorcycle and sidecar for them to get around in. In time, it would be swapped for a Rolls-Royce. Their only child, Gordon, was born in 1920.

Like every other British aviation company, Supermarine struggled when government money dried up after the First World War. It experimenting with diversifying into everything from manufacturing cars and toilet seats to running an airline — a division over which Scott-Paine ended up leaving the company in 1923.This did not impact Mitchell's career. In 1920, he became the company's chief designer at the age of 25, appointed to the post by Supermarine's new co-owner, a rakish ex-naval man by the name of Commander James Bird who had a penchant for the ladies and a discrete steam yacht out on Southampton Water upon which to entertain them.

Mitchell's first creation as chief designer was the prize-winning amphibian Supermarine Seagull, which sold in large quantities to both the RAF and the Royal Australian Air Force. Mitchell would go on to create 23 other designs for Supermarine during his twenty year career, including the Sea Eagle and Swan passenger planes, the Southampton (the first metal-hulled flying boat), the Walrus and the Stranraer. He became such an integral part of Supermarine that, when it was purchased by Vickers in 1928, one of the stipulations of the deal was that Mitchell would stay on in Southampton . Indeed, it's widely believed that Vickers purchased Supermarine mainly to obtain Mitchell's skills.

THE SCHNEIDER TROPHY

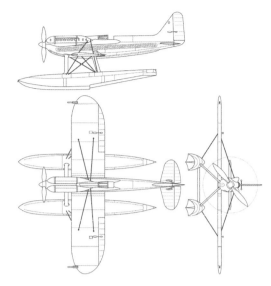

The Schneider Trophy competition was set up by a rich French aviation enthusiast and arms merchant, Jacques Schneider, in 1912. The idea was to encourage progress in aviation design, but it very quickly became a rip-roaring celebration and spectacle of speed, power and prestige as seaplanes roared around a triangular course over the sea. It was just the sort of thing that would attract the enthusiasm of Scott-Paine, beginning Supermarine's association with the contest that was to continue long after his departure. Mitchell shared Scott-Paine's enthusiasm for speed and became an essential part of Supermarine's Schneider team.

The Bay of Naples was decided up on the venue for the 1922 race. By now, Mussolini's fascists had assumed power in Italy and there was a keen desire to see the fascists humiliated before crowds of up to quarter of a million spectators. It was R.J. Mitchell and Supermarine who duly delivered the knockout blow to Mussolini, with their Supermarine Sea Lion II biplane securing victory at an average speed of 145.7mph.

By 1926, the Schneider Trophy had taken on a distinctly

militaristic air. All the pilots taking part were from their countries armed forces. There was no room for amateurs and enthusiasts any more. The Italians won the 1926 competition, held in Norfolk, Virginia, only stoking up the tension now evident between fascist Italy and the free nations. They could not be allowed to win again.

Despite the home advantage enjoyed by the Italians when the 1927 contest was staged in Venice, it was Britain who took First Place with a Supermarine S5 designed by Mitchell achieving a staggering 281.28mph average speed. British designs also took second and third place, thoroughly spoiling Mussolini's day and securing Great Britain a reputation as a world leader in aviation.

✛ L-R: British team for Schneider Trophy race 1929; Supermarine S.5, 1927; Supermarine S.5 Schneider Cup Racer N219 TOP: Line drawing of the Supermarine S-6B

✛ S.5 Winner of the Schneider Trophy at Venice in 1927

There was no contest held in 1928, but the Schneider Trophy returned in 1929 over the Solent — indisputably Supermarine's home ground. This time, Britain's entry was the S6, designed by Mitchell again and this time taking full advantage of the new Rolls-Royce R-Type V-12 military engine. On the ground, the crew working with the S6 included Aircraftsman T.E. Lawrence — Lawrence of Arabia. It was another resounding victory for the British entrant, with the S6 achieving average speeds of 328.63mph — over forty miles faster than its Italian competitor. The S6 broke the world speed record just days later, achieving 357.7mph. All thought immediately went to the 1931 contest. If the British team could win three times in a row, they would keep the trophy. There was supreme confidence in Supermarine and Mitchell to deliver that final knockout blow. And then the British government decided not to take part.

There was no contest in 1930, but by the time the 1931 competition rolled around the British Labour government had not shifted its position. Mired in a deepening recession, British politicians resented spending money on such a flippery as seaplane racing. Noting the increasing military involvement in the Schneider Trophy, many also took exception to spending money on what could be perceived as advancing weapons of war. RAF pilots were also expressly forbidden from taking part. Utopianism and pacifism trumped patriotism and achievement. *'Government blunder. Public astounded,'* roared the headlines on the Daily Mail, but Prime Minister Ramsay MacDonald refused to budge and his chancellor, Sir Philip Snowden, sneered that the Schneider Trophy was merely a manifestation of horrid jingoism and nationalism and only promoted *'pernicious rivalry between nations.'*

Salvation came in the form of one Dame Lucy Houston, a humble chorus girl turned suffragette turned society

hostess. Lucy — also known variously as Fanny or Poppy — had secured wealth for herself by seducing very rich older men across Europe. Her latest husband, the M.P. Sir Robert Paterson Houston, had conveniently died in mysterious circumstances on board his luxury yacht just two years after he had married Lucy, leaving her fabulously wealthy (she may well have been the richest woman in England) and free to spend as she wished. Dame Lucy Houston knew what she liked and what she didn't like, and one of the things she despised most in the world was a Labour government. To humiliate the one presently in power, she donated £100,000 to Supermarine to build a winning seaplane. Ramsay MacDonald was suitably humiliated, and Supermarine suitably delighted.

The government relented and allowed RAF pilots to take part in the Schneider Trophy and so it was that in September 1931, Flight-Lieutenant J.M. Boothman whipped around the Solent circuit on a Supermarine S6B, achieving a new record average speed of 379.5mph and securing the Schneider Trophy for Britain in perpetuity. Mitchell's design went on to smash the 400mph barrier and achieve a new world speed record barely a few weeks later. He himself was awarded a CBE.

What very few — including governments and military leaders — understood at the time was that the Schneider Trophy was not at heart about seaplanes or even seaplane development, or sport or spectacle. It was about speed, and developing thoroughbred new engines capable of powering sleek airframes ever faster. When designers built new Schneider seaplanes, they were in actuality refining and defining tomorrow's fighter aircraft. Not that would have mattered much to the British government. They believed that it was the bomber that would decide any future war in the air. Fighter planes were obsolete and would be simply swept aside like small buzzing insects as the mighty bomber formations filled the skies.

✛ Supermarine Rolls-Royce S6B seaplane, 1931

THE TYPE 224

Given the prevailing thinking that only bombers mattered and that fighters were obsolete, and given that government funding of the RAF was now at an all-time low due to pacifism and the Depression, it must have come as something of a shock to the British aviation industry when, in October 1931, the Air Ministry issued Specification F7/30 — a request for a new fighter aircraft.

F7/30 roughly coincided with Hugh Trenchard resigning as head of the RAF and being replaced by Sir John Salmond. Salmond was less wedded to the idea of bomber deterrence than his predecessor. Moreover, the British military aviation world now contained more than a few rebels. They included ex-fighter pilot Sir Hugh Dowding, now the Member for Supply and Research on the Air Council and Director of Technical Development Group

Captain Henry Cave-Brown-Cave. Papers had begun to emerge from the Air Ministry decrying orthodox thinking, revaluating the fighter aircraft and looking to the Schneider Trophy designs as proof that a new generations of fighter could result in something very exceptional indeed.

F7/30 called for an all-metal day and night fighter carrying four .303 machine guns, capable of 195mph at 15,000 feet, a minimum ceiling of 28,000 feet and able to land at speeds less than 60mph. There was no stipulation as to what engine had to be used or whether the fighter should be a monoplane or biplane.

Given Supermarine's stunning success in designing high speed, high performance aircraft for the Schneider Trophy, the company was considered by far the favourite to win. Mired in the depths of recession, all seven British aviation companies taking part fell upon F7/30 with some degree of

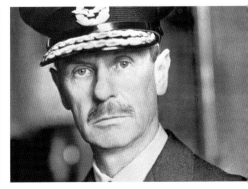

✛ L-R: TYPE 224; C.W.A. Scott (Pilot) and Sir John Salmond after Salmond's tour of northern Australia advising the RAAF on Aerial defence; Hugh Dowding TOP: TYPE 224

desperation. The opportunity could have resulted in radical thinking and spectacular design breakthroughs but — so desperate were the companies to secure the contract — that every single one of them decided to play it safe. The result was a glut of mediocrity.

Supermarine was the only company to submit a monoplane design, but there the innovation ended. For once, Mitchell's genius seemed to have abandoned him. Supermarine started work on a design they called the Type 224. The Type 224 brought with it problems right from the start. These centred around the 600hp Rolls Royce Goshawk engine selected by Mitchell to power the plane. The Goshawk required a complex and extensive cooling system, part of which needed to extend out into the wings and the undercarriage. This meant that both the wing and undercarriage design had to be seriously compromised. The undercarriage was bulky and could not retract, and the inverted gull wing was thick and inelegant. To add insult to injury, the engine cooling system could never be made

to work properly.. The compromised wing design further ended up with no flaps included, making the aircraft difficult to land at low speed or at night.

The Type 224 underwent its first test flight in February 1934 with test pilot 'Mutt' Summers at the controls. It failed to impress, achieving a disappointing 228mph in level flight and taking a tortoise-like 9.5 minutes to climb to 15,000ft. It was evident from the start that the 224 was a failure. No tinkering by Mitchell could save it. Throughout, the project ran long and it ran late. The Air Ministry thought this *'most disappointing.'* There had been vague thoughts of naming the Type 224 'Spitfire' — but it never stuck. It was as if the company itself could not raise sufficient enthusiasm for its own design

The Type 224 was eventually rejected and the Ministry settled for the Gloster Gladiator, which became the last RAF biplane fighter. They were not happy in their decision and talked of having to 'apply the screw' to British companies in

future. In 1934, they even looked, quite seriously, at buying Polish PZ24 fighters if British designs could not impress them.

THE TYPE 224 PROTOTYPE WAS SHOT TO DEATH ON A FIRING RANGE IN SUFFOLK IN 1937.

BROUGHT LOW

Mitchell, famed for the grace and elegance of his designs, had delivered an ungainly chunk of an aeroplane. What had gone wrong?

Voices rushed to defend Mitchell. His failure they said had been due to his lack of faith in the F7/30 specifications, or perhaps nerves at delivering his first military design. More critical voices thought that Mitchell had approached the project with too much over-confidence and was paying the price of conceit.

Through all the conjecture, the support and the rivalry, no-one knew what R.J. Mitchell was really going through. Mitchell had begun to feel unwell in late 1932 and after several months of illness finally saw his doctor. The outcome was not good. Tests revealed he was suffering from rectal cancer. In August 1933, he underwent an emergency operation. His rectum was removed and he was forced to use a colostomy bag, which he fitted to himself with a device of his own design. Mitchell was off sick from Supermarine for months, but eventually made it back into the Supermarine offices early in 1934. He told no-one, but he proved more difficult to work with than ever. Being in almost constant pain made him aggressive in meetings, One colleague, looking back with hindsight said, *'He was in shocking distress a lot of the time.'*

A NEW THREAT

The failure of the F7/30 project played out against a backdrop of increasing international tensions. The Geneva Disarmament Conference, at which Britain had been pushing for 'air disarmament', started to fall apart in 1933 when the German delegation pulled out. That same month, Germany withdrew from the League of Nations, and suddenly warplanes started to matter. A strong RAF was needed, if only as a deterrent. Britain now needed more planes — and better planes.

LEFT: The Westland F.7/30 fighter prototype K 2891

L-R: The Westland F.7/30 fighter; German delegation at the Geneva Disarmament Conference in 1933; Political cartoon of the World Disarmament Conference

PER ARDUA
AD ASTRA...

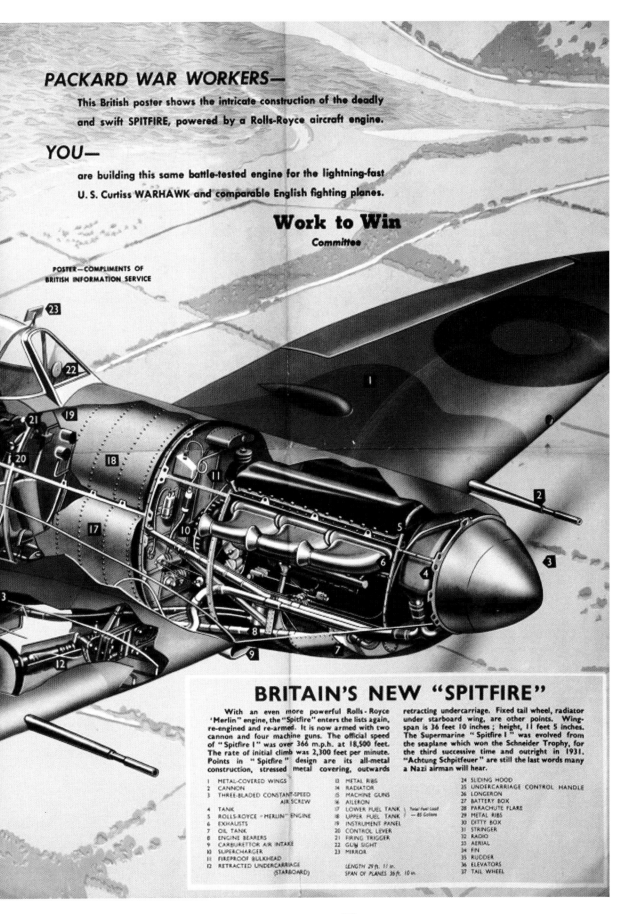

PACKARD WAR WORKERS—

This British poster shows the intricate construction of the deadly and swift SPITFIRE, powered by a Rolls-Royce aircraft engine.

YOU—

are building this same battle-tested engine for the lightning-fast U. S. Curtiss WARHAWK and comparable English fighting planes.

Work to Win
Committee

POSTER—COMPLIMENTS OF
BRITISH INFORMATION SERVICE

BRITAIN'S NEW "SPITFIRE"

With an even more powerful Rolls-Royce 'Merlin' engine, the "Spitfire" enters the lists again, re-engined and re-armed. It is now armed with two cannon and four machine guns. The official speed of "Spitfire I" was over 366 m.p.h. at 18,500 feet. The rate of initial climb was 2,300 feet per minute. Points in "Spitfire" design are its all-metal construction, stressed metal covering, outwards retracting undercarriage. Fixed tail wheel, radiator under starboard wing, are other points. Wing-span is 36 feet 10 inches; height, 11 feet 5 inches. The Supermarine "Spitfire I" was evolved from the seaplane which won the Schneider Trophy, for the third successive time and outright in 1931. "Achtung Schpitfeuer" are still the last words many a Nazi airman will hear.

1 METAL-COVERED WINGS	13 METAL RIBS	24 SLIDING HOOD
2 CANNON	14 RADIATOR	25 UNDERCARRIAGE CONTROL HANDLE
3 THREE-BLADED CONSTANT-SPEED AIR SCREW	15 MACHINE GUNS	26 LONGERON
	16 AILERON	27 BATTERY BOX
4 TANK	17 LOWER FUEL TANK ⎫ Total Fuel Load	28 PARACHUTE FLARE
5 ROLLS-ROYCE "MERLIN" ENGINE	18 UPPER FUEL TANK ⎭ — 85 Gallons	29 METAL RIBS
6 EXHAUSTS	19 INSTRUMENT PANEL	30 DITTY BOX
7 OIL TANK	20 CONTROL LEVER	31 STRINGER
8 ENGINE BEARERS	21 FIRING TRIGGER	32 RADIO
9 CARBURETTOR AIR INTAKE	22 GUN SIGHT	33 AERIAL
10 SUPERCHARGER	23 MIRROR	34 FIN
11 FIREPROOF BULKHEAD		35 RUDDER
12 RETRACTED UNDERCARRIAGE (STARBOARD)	LENGTH 29 ft. 11 in.	36 ELEVATORS
	SPAN OF PLANES 36 ft. 10 in.	37 TAIL WHEEL

25

THE TYPE 300

Mitchell and his team knew that they could build something better than the Type 224. A new version, known as the Type 300, featured a retractable undercarriage, shorter wings, wing flaps and some innovations developed from Supermarine's Schneider racers. It wasn't enough. In July 1934, the Air Ministry turned the design down again.

Finally, Mitchell hit upon the key change he needed to make. He abandoned the Goshawk engine and turned instead to the new Rolls-Royce 790hp PV12. One day, Sir Henry Royce had boasted, this engine would be capable of 1,000hp. By 1935, it was producing 990hp — and one day soon the PV12 would become the Merlin. Mitchell was totally convinced by it.

More design changes followed. The revised Type 300 would now feature an enclosed cockpit and semi-elliptical wings designed to be thin, but sizeable enough to contain retracted

undercarriage, machine guns and ammunition. Initially, the aircraft was to have four .303 Browning machine guns, but this was increased to eight in 1935. It was thought that any fighter would have just one or two seconds with a bomber firmly in its sights and therefore it was desirable to pump as many bullets into the enemy aircraft as possible in that short time. An accurate two second burst with eight guns would see the enemy hit with a fusillade of 288 bullets. The Type 300 would be able to fire eight such bursts before needing to re-arm.` In the words of Sir Robert McLean, chairman of Vickers, the new aircraft would be a *'real killer fighter.'*

Vickers were impressed with Mitchell's thinking, and in November 1934 officially began to fund the project. The fighter enthusiasts in the Air Ministry liked it too — particularly Dowding and Cave-Brown-Cave — and in December 1934 they paid £10,000 towards the new Type 300's development. *'Delivery is urgently required,'* said the contract. A month later, they issued a new specification — F10/35 — deliberately written around the Type 300's anticipated capabilities.

What Mitchell and his team had envisaged was a powerful, short range fighter for the defence of Britain, intended to go up and claw an enemy bomber fleet from the skies. Tangling with other fighters was a secondary consideration, as it was thought that bombers would arrive unescorted. No enemy fighter — and by now this meant German — would have the range to escort them over the British Isles.

Somewhere along the way, the Type 300 became the Spitfire. The name was dreamed up by Head of Vickers Robert McLean, who had taken to calling his spirited young daughter Annie *'a little spitfire.'* When he heard, Mitchell said it was *'just the sort of bloody silly name they would choose.'* He wanted to call it the Supermarine Shrew.

✈ Sir Robert Mclean

✈ Sir Henry Royce

PER ARDUA AD ASTRA

FIRST FLIGHT

With the Air Ministry positively desperate for results now the great rival to the Spitfire, the Hawker Hurricane, made its first flight in November 1935. It had been hoped that the Prototype Spitfire would fly by October 1935. As it was, the prototype — K5054 — did not fly until 5 March 1936, and even then it was barely ready. It was Vickers' chief test pilot, Joseph 'Mutt' Summers, who took K5054 up from Eastleigh Airfield — now Southampton Airport — in the late afternoon. Mutt flew K5054 for eight minutes, putting it through a gentle testing before coming into land. As he climbed from the cockpit he said *'I don't want anything touched'.*

This has been interpreted as the Spitfire was perfect from its very first outing, but it was not what Mutt meant. He wanted to keep all the controls and instrumentation as they were to replicate conditions on his next test flight, which

occurred the next day and lasted for 23 minutes. Witnessing those early test flights, the men from the Air Ministry became very excited. Even the supremely dour Dowding admitted that *'the flying was highly satisfactory.'*

Jeffrey Quill, then Mutt's assistant, made his first Spitfire test flight on 26 March — and fell in love:

'...it was somewhat reminiscent of my old Bentley cruising in top gear...it evidently enjoyed flying... 'Here', I thought to myself, 'is a real lady.'

Amid all this, it was now R.J. Mitchell who was the Spitfire's greatest critic. The early test flights had seen the Spitfire only achieve 335 mph — not the 350mph he had been banking on. That meant that the Spitfire was not all that much faster than its rival the Hurricane. Given that the Hurricane was easier, faster and cheaper to build, the Spitfire could well ultimately face rejection by the Ministry. Mitchell raced to make improvements before the official

✈ British test pilot Jeffrey Quill (1913 — 1996) takes off in the Supermarine Spitfire prototype (K5054) for a press demonstration at Eastleigh Aerodrome, Hampshire, 18th June 1936

RAF air trials could begin, making changes in the rudder function, installing a new propeller and changing the cowlings and fairings. It worked. The next time Quill went up in K5054, he achieved 348mph in level flight and 380mph in a dive. *'I think we've got something here,'* he said rather chirpily after coming in to land.

K5054 was surrendered to RAF Martlesham to begin RAF trials on 26 May 1936. Large crowds gathered to watch as test pilot Humphrey Edwardes - Jones took her up at just after 5.30pm — and proceeded to nearly kill himself. After a faultless flight, Edwardes - Jones came into land, forgetting that the aircraft had a retractable undercarriage and that his wheels were still up. He remembered just in time. Upon landing safely, Edwardes - Jones rushed to the telephone to report to Sir Wilfrid Freeman at the Ministry. Freeman wanted to know if such an advanced plane was suitable to be flown by the grade of airmen the RAF were now recruiting. *'Yes,'* Edwardes - Jones assured him, *'provided they are given adequate instruction in the use of flaps and retracting undercarriage!'*

It was confirmation of the Air Ministry's desperation for the Spitfire that the decision to purchase the aircraft was based on that one hurried phone call. Just eight days later, Supermarine received an initial order for 310 Spitfires. The order specified that all 310 planes needed to be delivered by March 1939 and that the Ministry would pay £4,500 per Spitfire, not including the cost of the engine, radio or guns.

GOING PUBLIC

On 18 June 1936, the Spitfire made its first public appearance at a Vickers Open Day held at Eastleigh Aerodrome. Under two weeks later, K5054 stole the show at the 1936 Hendon Air Pageant. Magazines and newspapers, perhaps mindful of the perilous times, began to eulogise the Spitfire right from its debut, celebrating its speed and manoeuvrability. A legend was starting to be born.

A TERRIBLE LOSS

Throughout the latter part of 1936, it was evident to Mitchell that his cancer was returning, and now with a vengeance. He was forced to miss more and more meetings and was not capable of bearing his workload any more. In February 1937, he visited a London hospital to explore the possibility of a second operation — but the news was grim. Another operation was pointless. This time the cancer would very likely kill him in a matter of months. Mitchell set about getting his affairs in order and quit work officially that same month.

By March 1937, Mitchell's conditioned deteriorated further and relief could only be found in increasing doses of morphine. Despite his stricken condition, he made one last attempt to save himself. There were rumours that Austrian medicine had made progress in the treatments of some cancers and Mitchell flew out to meet one of the world's leading cancer specialists, Professor Freund, at his clinic. He spent a month at Freund's clinic but never had any real chance to recover. His cancer was too far advanced.

By the end of May 1937, Mitchell had returned home and spent what time he could in the gardens, looking out over the fishpond he loved so much. The end came soon. He slipped into a coma on 6 June and died on 11 June. Reginald Joseph Mitchell was forty-two years old. Following his funeral, he was cremated and interred at South Stoneham Cemetery. Three RAF planes flew past and dipped their wings in salute.

JOE SMITH

After Mitchell's death, the Spitfire project was taken up by Joe Smith, a native of Birmingham who would stay with the Spitfire and further develop its design and potential right through to the end of production. During that time, Smith would see the Spitfire through 24 different marks and forty variants. He has been called *'the Spitfire's forgotten designer.'*

TOO LITTLE, TOO LATE

Vickers and Supermarine had been delighted to have received an order for 310 Spitfires, and quickly set about deluding themselves that they could ever fulfil it.

At the Air Ministry, the Secretary of State for Air, the Viscount Swinton, had become so enamoured of the prospects of the Spitfire that he seriously considered increasing the initial order. After all, 600 Hurricanes had been ordered and that was a plane he personally considered inferior to the Spitfire. By January 1937 however, Viscount Swinton's enthusiasm was turning to alarm. He heard word that Supermarine would only deliver a handful of Spitfires in 1937, instead of the promised sixty. He kept turning to Robert McLean for reassurance — and got it. Everything was progressing splendidly, he promised. Behind the scenes, Supermarine were indeed struggling. Because of their limited capacity on the Southampton site and, because of the advanced machines required to build the Spitfire, they had subcontracted out part of the design — and some of their new partners had quality control and work ethics that did not meet Supermarine's finer standards. Even among the good ones, few had previous experience of aviation engineering or its particular needs. By 1938, Supermarine were subcontracting to almost 80 such firms. The elliptical wing design in particular proved a nightmare. Furthermore, Joe Smith's design team kept coming up with new improvements which needed to be incorporated into the production cycle. This meant changes on everything from the guns (and gunsight) to the wireless to the leading edge of the wings — and that was before Rolls-Royce introduced changes to the Merlin.

Now it was predicted that just four Spitfires would be delivered in December 1937 and less than fifteen during the whole first quarter of 1938. By summer, Vickers were admitting that they might only deliver a single Spitfire in December 1937. That delivery date got pushed back to February 1938. In the event, Supermarine managed to deliver six Spitfires in December 1937. The only problem was they had no wings. Vickers blamed the subcontractors, as had become established policy. Now the first complete Spitfire was promised for March 1938 — and would cost £7,000 instead of the £4,500 per plane as originally agreed.

The Air Ministry was starting to get the blame for what senior politicians regarded as a fiasco. In February 1938,

 JosephSmith

 Lord Swinton

Hitler annexed Austria. Despite their chronic problems, Supermarine received a further order for an additional 200 Spitfires as war fears intensified. By the end of March 1938, Supermarine had no less than thirty-five Spitfires in their hangars at Eastleigh. Spitfires with no wings it was true, but there they were. There was great joy when four pairs of wings duly arrived from a subcontractor and not some little haste in marrying them to the fuselages. Fingers were crossed that these would actually fit.

By May, Swinton was gone, torn down by an unholy parliamentary mix of hawks under Churchill and the Labour Party under Attlee. Sir Kingsley Wood took his place. On the day Swinton resigned, Jeffrey Quill took the very first complete production Spitfire — K9787 — up for its first air trial. It would be two more months before the Supermarine production lines produced another one.

FLATTERING LORD NUFFIELD

By May 1938, the unholy state of the Spitfire project provoked fierce debate and even calls for an inquiry in Parliament. Matters had reached crisis point. It was then that the new Secretary of State for Air surprised everybody. By his own admission, Sir Kingsley Wood knew next to nothing about aviation — but he did know a little something about business and businessmen. For some time, the government had been building 'shadow factories' as they geared up for war — either sponsoring new manufacturing plants to increase their capacity or getting other companies to produce their products for them. This process, which was sometimes heavy-handed at worst or insensitive at best, had alienated many of Britain's leading business moguls and they had consequently refused to co-operate.

Lord Nuffield, head of the Morris Corporation, was probably the most powerful example. Viscount Swinton had put his nose out of joint and not shown sufficient respect. Now Wood proposed a very different approach — rank flattery. Wood met Nuffield and proposed they build a massive new factory. Its first task would be to turn out 1,000 Spitfires, thereby enjoying the largest government order ever given to British aviation. Nuffield would receive £2 million to build this super factory and a further £7 million for the thousand Spitfires. The plan was so huge, so ambitious that Lord Nuffield quite had his head turned and was on board in double quick time.

Despite the government being royally ripped off over the land purchase price, a large 135 acre factory was soon under construction in Castle Bromwich in Birmingham, partly encompassing an old sewage works. The Morris Corporation promised to turn out 60 Spitfires per week once the factory was complete. Almost all government hopes now rested with Nuffield: At Supermarine's Southampton works, they were currently trying to work out what to do with 78 Spitfire fuselages and less than five pairs of wings...

✝ Sir Kingsley Wood

✚ William Morris

INTO SERVICE

By the very end of July 1938 there were four completed
Spitfires sitting in Southampton. These were duly flown to
Martlesham for RAF testing. On 4 August, Spitfire K9789
was delivered to 19 Squadron at Duxford by Jeffrey Quill.
19 Squadron were currently flying Gloster Gladiators and
the sight of the Spitfire against the flights of biplanes left
no one in any doubt that the future had at last arrived. But
had it arrived in time? The Munich Crisis and *'Peace in
our Time'* was only a month away. At Munich, amid other
shameful acts, Chamberlain would sell out the Czech
people in order to gain more time to re-arm and to see
more Spitfires come off the production line.

⊕ L-R: Gloster Gladiators MAIN IMAGE: A Spitfire of No. 19 Squadron is refuelled at Fowlmere, near Duxford, September 1940

OUT OF LOVE

As Germany annexed the Sudetenland, the Air Ministry — and many others — were rapidly falling out of love with the Spitfire. It was late, it was over-budget and it was in danger of becoming obsolete even before it could appear in any significant numbers.

Other problems revealed themselves. In test flights, it was found that the Spitfire's Brownings would freeze up and fail, just at the altitude it could expect to intercept enemy bomber formations. The problem could be solved by pumping in heat from the engine, but this meant refashioning the wings to allow for the pipework — no small job. When he heard about this, CAS of the RAF Sir Cyril Newall was utterly furious and warned that the Spitfire might well be *'useless.'*

The Air Ministry, despairing of the whole Spitfire project, started looking around for a replacement design. They considered three other designs — The Camm Fighter (which eventually became the Hawker Typhoon), the Westland Whirlwind and the Bristol Beaufighter. Of them all, the Ministry and the RAF were most taken by the Whirlwind. By the end of the year, it was seriously suggested that the Castle Bromwich plant — when it was finally ready — should immediately be given over to building Whirlwinds, and to hell with the Spitfire. More cautious minds feared that the Whirlwind would come into production too late and it was best to nurse the Spitfire through its many and varied problems and to see it as merely a stop-gap until something better came along.

✈ Vickers Supermarine Works, Southampton

✠ L-R: Sir Cyril Newall (centre); Beaufighter; Westland Whirlwind prototype TOP: Hawker_Typhoon

TROUBLE AT THE MILL

While the Spitfire's future was being debated, it became clear that the new Spitfire Factory at Castle Bromwich was in serious trouble. By September 1938, construction of the facility was well behind schedule and it would be a considerable time before it could produce its first Spitfire. By the start of 1939, the cost of building Castle Bromwich — which was still nowhere near complete — had ballooned from £2 million to £4 million. Anxious parties were told to be silent in case they upset Lord Nuffield — while in March that year the Nazis invaded the remaining part of Czechoslovakia that they had not conquered earlier.

By the beginning of July 1939, Supermarine's Southampton plant however had finally managed to deliver 240 Spitfires from the original order of 310 placed back in 1936. It had solved many issues with its subcontractors and was paying its workforce a small fortune in overtime payments.

✈ Factory workers at Vickers Supermarine Works, Southampton drilling parts for the Spitfire

✈ L-R & TOP: Spitfire Factory, Castle Bromwich, Birmingham

FROM DESPERATION TO DUNKIRK

WAR

When war was declared on Germany on 3 September 1939, the air raid sirens sounded — but it was a false alarm. The skies over London were empty. The predicted mass bomber fleets delivering annihilation from the sky never materialised. Neither side dared and, — in truth — neither side was capable. In Britain, the heavy bomber projects were well behind schedule while the Luftwaffe had not bothered with heavy bombers and had fashioned a bomber fleet largely to support ground troops.

At the beginning of September 1939, the RAF had 270 Spitfires and 400 Hurricanes in service. The Spitfires comprised ten squadrons. 306 Spitfires had been delivered by Supermarine in Southampton by now, but over 10% had been written off in training accidents. It was an ominous sign — and no one yet knew how the Spitfire would fare in air combat. It was still largely considered a 'stop gap' until something better came along.

THE BATTLE OF BARKING CREEK

Spitfires achieved their first kills less than a week after war broke out. Unfortunately, the first two planes they shot down were 56 Squadron Hawker Hurricanes. On 6 September 1939, Spitfires from 94 Squadron at Hornchurch were vectored after unidentified aircraft approaching the Essex coast and pounced from above, blowing two Hurricanes out of the sky and killing one of their pilots. The pilots responsible were arrested as soon as they landed and subsequently court martialled. They were acquitted and the tragic incident led to the fitting of 'Identification Friend or Foe' (IFF) radar signalling equipment in all RAF aircraft.

✝ TOP: John Freeborn ABOVE: Downed Hurricane from The Battle of Barking Creek

✛ A newsboy carries a poster proclaiming Britain's declaration of war on Germany, the Embankment, London, 3rd September 1939

EARLY KILLS

...Spitfires are wonderful machines and ...the Huns hate them.'
A.C. Broome, Air Ministry, October 1939

Thankfully, Spitfires did not just prove themselves deadly against friendly aircraft. On 16 October 1939, nine Ju.88 bombers went hunting the battleship *Hood,* rumoured to be at anchor in the Firth of Forth. The *Hood* was elsewhere so the bombers went after two RN cruisers instead, with little effect. As the Ju.88s turned for home, they were hit from above by Spitfires from 602 and 603 Squadron. Two Ju.88s went down in the Forth Estuary — the first proper kills of the war for RAF Fighter Command. The next day, three Spitfires jumped a lone Heinkel 111 25 miles off the coast of Whitby and brought it down. The enemy crew survived and paddled their dinghy ashore to become the first Germans taken prisoner over Britain.

A NEW ROLE

In September 1939, ex-MI6 man Wing Commander Sydney

Cotton was given the task of establishing a unit to fly long range photo-reconnaissance missions. Being based at Heston, it naturally became known as the Heston Flight. Originally it was planned to use Blenheim's in the role but — even as early as 1939 — the RAF were beginning to realise that the Blenheim was an underperformer and would be very unlikely to avoid interception by enemy fighters. Indeed, in 42 sorties, the unit lost eight Blenheims and the photographs they were able to snatch under such threat were poor. Cotton instead requested and received two Spitfires. These were quickly modified to carry extra fuel (nearly three times as much as a standard Spitfire) and cameras in the wings instead of guns. These two aircraft were designated PR Mk.1As.

Photoreconnaissance was never a role envisioned for the Spitfire but it quickly proved more than up to the task. In mid-November, one of these Spitfires was flown out to France to take part in the unit's very first mission — to film the fortifications around the German city of Aachen. Unfortunately, it filmed Belgium instead. Three days later though, the specially modified Spitfire succeeded in filming German border specifications. From then on, Spitfires

✈ Supermarine Spitfire I (K9787) in flight from Eastleigh

✈ L-R: H.M.S. Hood; Donald Finlay of No. 41 Squadron, Observer Corp; Heston Aerodrome TOP: Ju.88 bomber

were used in photoreconnaissance roles throughout the war and in numerous theatres and a number of Spitfire marks and variants would be produced especially for photoreconnaissance duties.

MORE PRODUCTION PROBLEMS

By the first quarter of 1940, 40 Spitfires per month were being produced by Supermarine's Southampton Facilities. By contrast, Castle Bromwich — initially supposed to start producing sixty Spitfires a week aircraft from February 1939 — was rescheduled to start production in April 1940. April came but no Spitfires with it. Despite having a workforce more than twice the size of Supermarine in Southampton, not a single aircraft was produced. The politicians were cowed by Lord Nuffield's reputation and, when they were brave enough to enquire of His Lordship as to what was wrong, Nuffield would blame drawings supplied by Supermarine, or new design modifications or whatever else he could think of. Nuffield, who had started life as a bicycle repair man before mass producing motor cars, simply had no understanding of the complex requirements of the aviation industry and the pressure was starting to get to him. The man who had once bankrolled Mosley's British Union of Fascists in its infancy and who had an unhealthy obsession with his own voluminous flatulence

(woe betide those who had an extended meeting with him), was now coming apart under the strain of trying to produce Spitfires. His exhausted works manager at Castle Bromwich, Oliver Boden, then inconveniently fell dead in March 1940, no doubt much to his Lordship's displeasure.

PHONEY NO MORE

At the start of April 1940, the Phoney War ended. Germany invaded Norway and Denmark. The British campaign in Norway went badly and the Chamberlain government convulsed and then collapsed. Winston Churchill came into power at the head of a national coalition government — and things started to change very rapidly.

Churchill brought in Sir Archibald Sinclair as Secretary of State for Air and on 14 May 1940 placed his good friend and proprietor of the Daily Express, Lord Beaverbrook, in the new position of Head of the Ministry of Aircraft Production. A gnome-like Canadian possessed of great energy but little empathy, Beaverbrook was despised in many quarters. *'Evil'* was how Head of the BBC Lord Reith described him, while Spitfire legend Alex Henshaw thought him *'an unpleasant bastard.'* Beaverbrook was a rule-breaking, disrespectful attack dog, and now Churchill set him upon the British aircraft industry.

Beaverbrook saw clearly that what Britain most needed at this time was an abundance of fighters and he deliberately disrupted bomber production to bring the fighters in. Just three days after taking office, Beaverbrook also decided to sort out the Castle Bromwich debacle once and for all and picked up the phone to Lord Nuffield. Nuffield predictably launched in to a hard-nosed defence listing all the problems he was experiencing. Then he tried to bluff Beaverbrook with the ultimate threat:

'Perhaps you would like me to give up control of the Spitfire factory?'

To which Beaverbrook immediately replied:

'Nuffield, that's very generous of you. I accept!' — and hung up…

It was reported by office staff that Nuffield went quite pale. His speech entirely deserted him and, when he had sufficiently recovered, he sank into the most grievous of sulks. Beaverbrook meanwhile straightaway called up Vickers and told them they were now in charge of Castle Bromwich. Southampton men were despatched to Birmingham to bring order to the chaos within hours.

As Vickers fought to bring order to Castle Bromwich, Beaverbrook asked Sir Richard Fairey to produce a detailed report on the factory. He found fault with virtually everything, but saved his greatest criticisms for the workforce. The workers, Fairey reported, came in and went home as they pleased and showed scant respect for their managers. They went on strike at the drop of a hat, despite being paid far

✈ L-R: The Secretary of State for Air, Sir Archibald Sinclair (in civilian raincoat); Churchill Coalition Government; Lord Beaverbrook

✈ Spitfire landing at an airfield

more than their fellows in Southampton and idled whenever they could get away with it. In the chaos, shop floor fraud and pilfering was widespread. What's more, they were using selective stoppages in strategic parts of the production line to prevent Spitfires from rolling off the production line in favour of yet more pay increases. Fairey was so alarmed by the workforce that he feared their disruptive indolence would spread to other factories, and recommended that they all be threatened with conscription if they didn't mend their ways. He was not alone in his view. One of the Supermarine team despatched to Castle Bromwich accused left wingers in the factory of actions that *'bordered on treason'* by deliberately sabotaging Spitfire production. Hitler was widely seen as a friend to the Soviet Union at this point in the war, and many on the Left saw Britain by virtue of its allegiances to capitalism and Imperialism as the true enemy on the international stage.

The sackings started in June 1940. 184 troublemakers and lazybones were gone by 8 August.

Spitfires started to come off the Castle Bromwich production line at long last. 23 Spitfires appeared in July 1940, 37 the following month, 56 in September and 195 in October. Castle Bromwich was finally coming good — and would eventually turn out more than 13,000 Spitfires.

BLITZKRIEG

At Dawn on 10 May 1940, Hitler finally unleashed 'The Blitzkrieg'. Two armoured corps and paratrooper units, with close air support provided by the Luftwaffe, burst into Belgium and the Netherlands. French forces — along with significant elements of the British Expeditionary Force — moved forward into Belgium to confront them. It was a trap. To their east, a mass of German armour poured out of the Ardennes Forest and swiftly powered their way westward across France to the sea. The Allies to the north were swiftly cut off and surrounded in a perfectly executed pincer movement.

There were no fighting Spitfire squadrons stationed in France at the time. Fighter cover was left to the Hurricane. Just days after the Blitzkrieg began, French Prime Minister Paul Reynaud phoned Winston Churchill and told him c'est fini. '*We have been defeated,*' he said. '*We are beaten. We have lost the battle.*' Churchill was stunned and — in an embarrassed effort to stop Reynaud crying, promised him more British resources, including ten Spitfire squadrons.

This was vigorously and immediately opposed by Air Chief Marshal Hugh Dowding, who was now Head of RAF Fighter Command, having been placed in the job because no-one liked him and because in the far off days of 1936, fighter

✈ Paul Reynaud

✈ Spitfire in flight

planes had been considered the lowest of the low. Committing extra fighters to the fight for France would mean a weakened home defence force. When the Germans came — and they surely would — Britain would need every fighter aircraft it could muster to meet the German bomber armadas.

This was not what Churchill wanted to hear, but when he flew to France to assess the situation for himself, he found its military and government in a state of almost total chaos — and realised the war there was indeed all but lost. Returning home, he found himself agreeing with Dowding — much to his own personal displeasure — and broke his promise of committing Spitfire squadrons to the fight.

OPERATION DYNAMO

'I thumbed the trigger button just once, twice. I smelt the cordite fumes blowing back from my Brownings as the 1,200 squirts a minute from each of them went into him. I saw the little spurts of flame as the tracers struck…I saw a burst of flame and smoke from his engine, and then he was going down in a twirling spin of black smoke.'

Pilot Officer Johnny Allen, 54 Squadron, on shooting down a Bf 109 over Dunkirk.

By 24 May, German panzers had reached the Channel ports

and Britain was looking to evacuate and rescue what it could of its troops. The plan was made to concentrate retreating forces on the port of Dunkirk and then to evacuate them by sea. It was hoped that, at most, they might rescue as many as 40,000 men. On 26 May, the Allied evacuation at Dunkirk began. Looking on, the Head of the Luftwaffe, Hermann Goering chuckled and said '*I hope the Tommies are good swimmers!*' Back in England, the fighters of 11 Group (London and the South-East) under Air Vice Marshal Keith Park were tasked with flying across the Channel and providing air cover. It was now that the Spitfire would be truly tested for the first time, coming hard up against its principal rival, the Messerschmitt Bf.109.

Flying over Dunkirk, Spitfires were invariably short on fuel and time. They could not be accurately vectored on to the German bomber squadrons inbound for the port and had to sight the enemy themselves and then decide tactics on the spot. However, when Spitfires found the Luftwaffe, they proved effective against everything they met, from Stuka dive bombers and Ju.88s to their Bf.109 and Bf.110 fighter escorts. The first Spitfire aces were born over Dunkirk — including the New Zealander Alan Deere and Squadron Leader James Leathart (nicknamed 'The Prof' because he had been to University). One German officer reported, *'the enemy fighters pounced on us with the fury of maniacs!'* Luftwaffe pilots had previously referred to themselves as 'Cowboys' and enemy aircraft as 'Indians.' Now, the warning cry of '*Achtung Indianer!*' over their RT was

replaced by '*Achtung Schpitfeuer!*' — a phrase that was to linger in the British psyche for many decades. German fighter pilots were shocked in particular by the Spitfire's turning ability, something they simply could not match.

Spitfire pilots learned many valuable lessons from their dogfights over Dunkirk. These included getting their guns harmonized to deliver a concentrated burst of fire at 250 yards rather than the recommended 400 yards and to ignore the niceties of deflection shooting, which few could master. The order of the day was to get in fast, get up close, deliver maximum firepower and then climb away again. They also learned that the recommended Vic formation of three Spitfires led to all kinds of problems in real combat, and soon came to adopt the 'Finger Four' formation, one that was preferred by Luftwaffe fighter pilots.

Dynamo finally came to an end on 3 June. During the evacuation, Fighter Command had flown over 2,740 combat sorties and the evacuation had been a resounding success. The military had hoped to rescue at best 40,000 troops. Instead, 224,686 British and 121,445 French and Belgian troops had been plucked from the beaches and brought home. Losses were inevitable. The RAF lost 38 Spitfires over Dunkirk as well as 61 Hurricanes and eighty valuable pilots. The Luftwaffe suffered 132 losses.

ALONE

The French government formally surrendered to the Nazis on 22 June. For Dowding, the news came as a relief. His aircraft and his men would no longer have to be sacrificed in a battle that was clearly lost. '*Thank God, now we are alone,*' he famously said. The RAF was still in a parlous state, though. Dowding always believed he needed 52 fighter squadrons to defend Britain. He had significantly fewer.

✠ L-R: The new General Field Marshals of the Luftwaffe, from left to right: Erhard Milch, Hugo Sperrle, Adolf Hitler, Reichsmarschall Hermann Göring and Albert Kesselring; Sir Keith Park; Robert Stanford-Tuck — Alan Deere — 'Sailor' Malan — James Leathart

✠ Spitfire landing at an airfield

SPITFIRE VERSUS B F.109

Dogfighting over Dunkirk had revealed a number of ways in which a Bf.109 could enjoy an advantage over the Spitfire. The answer, it was found, was to convert Spitfires to constant-speed, variable pitch airscrew propellers from the two-pitch propellers found on most Spitfire Mk.Is. With a speed possible only in wartime, Dowding ordered the conversions to begin on 22 June. It would improve Spitfire performance in combat just a little — but just a little might be just enough. Conversion work started just three days later, with over twenty aircraft a day converted. The air war over Dunkirk had also revealed other weaknesses that were rapidly dealt with. A shield was constructed over the main fuel tank forward of the cockpit to deflect bullets. Armour plating was fitted to the rear of the pilot seat, a laminated glass shield in front of the cockpit canopy and a rear view mirror fitted to stop the pilot having to look over his shoulder in combat.

CANNON FIRE

One big advantage enjoyed by the Bf.109 was being fitted with two cannon. Eight Brownings, all too often, could not get the job done and experts believed that it was taking an average of 4,500 Browning rounds to bring down just one enemy aircraft.

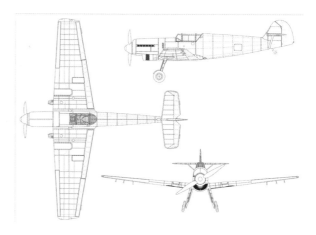

It was well understood that the answer was cannon capable of firing explosive shells. In combat, it was believed that a single cannon would have the firepower equivalent to twelve .303 machine guns.

In 1938, tests had started with the 20mm Hispano cannon. The initial tests, with two Hispanos mounted on a Spitfire, were not encouraging. The cannon needed to be fitted awkwardly on their sides and the cannon shells showed a tendency to misfeed and then jam the gun, especially during violent manoeuvres. If a cannon did jam, firing the remaining one was enough to throw the entire aircraft off to one side.

By June 1940, it was hoped that these problems had been ironed out and the Cannon Spitfire, designated Mk.IB, was given to 19 Squadron to fly. 19 Squadron first saw frontline combat in

✝ Line drawing of a Messerschmitt Bf 109

✠ Messerschmitt Bf 109

August 1940 — and their Hispano cannon let them down almost immediately. On 16 August, in the heat of combat, the cannon failed on six out of seven Spitfires. The squadron suffered more catastrophic cannon problems throughout the rest of the month and, by the start of September, were practically begging to have their old eight Browning Spitfires back.

It would not be until November 1940, after the Battle of Britain, that problems with the Hispanos had been largely overcome and they could be mounted on Spitfires with some confidence. A combination of two cannon and four Brownings became the standard configuration for armament on the Spitfire 'B' Wing.

HEARTS AND MINDS

The Germans first discovered what the Spitfire could do in the skies above Dunkirk — and so did the British. Criticism of the aircraft was suddenly and forcefully muted. This was no stopgap fighting machine. The situation was now catastrophic, with France gone, the Army in a state of disrepair, the RAF well below strength and Germany planning its move on Britain. It was one of the darkest hours ever experienced by the British nation — but at least it had the Spitfire. The Spitfire gave the public an increasing sense of hope. It became in just a few short months, a wonder weapon in the hearts and minds of the public, something that might save them from the coming invasion. The Spitfire was starting to become a legend — a very useful legend.

SPITFIRES FOR THE PEOPLE

' (The Spitfire)…probably had a greater impact on the will of the people to survive and put more heart into their morale, when it was at its lowest ebb, than anything created in modern times.' — Alex Henshaw

Lord Beaverbrook was more than Churchill's attack dog. He was more than the man who saved Spitfire production. He

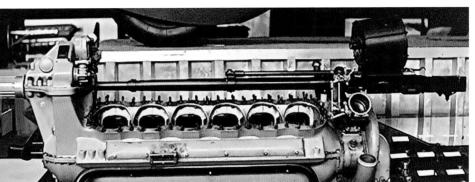

✚ L-R: Mounting position 20 mm cannon in HS12 Ydrs motor. The cylinders have been removed for a better view; Oldsmobile licence-produced the Hispano-Suiza HS.404 cannon TOP: 20 mm Hispano-Suiza Mk 5 cannon

was also a press baron — and he had a nose for a great story and an insight into what the public needed and wanted. It was Beaverbrook who understood the public's growing love of — and faith in — the Spitfire before virtually anyone else — and he decided to use it.

He started out with a public appeal for housewives to donate their aluminium pots and pans to help build Spitfires. The metal was utterly useless for Spitfire production, but that didn't matter. Now, everyone had something they could contribute. Now everyone could help put a Spitfire up in the sky.

The Women's Voluntary Service set up collection points, and housewives came to donate by the handful and by the

pram-full. For their donation, they were rewarded by a little label badge saying 'Shareholder in the Spitfire'. Slogans were painted on walls or chalked on blackboards at collection dumps saying things like '*I saw your kettle chasing a German bomber over Kent the other day*' and '*Out of the frying pan, into the (Spit)fire.*'

Beaverbrook went still further with 'The Spitfire Fund'. For £5,000 you could now sponsor your own Spitfire and have your name painted on the side. Britons could also buy Spitfire components, ranging from a £200 Browning to a sixpenny rivet.

Groups not just in Britain but throughout the Empire started their own funds. '*I'll fly it if you buy it,*' promised an RAF pilot

✝ LEFT: Segregated Scrap Fights Again! Poster; RIGHT: RAF Royal Air Force propaganda poster 'Wings for victory', Wings for Victory' fund raising weeks during which people were asked to contribute money for a Spitfire

from the wall poster. By the first week in August 1940, over £2.5 million had been raised for Spitfires. There were funds set up by women's prisons, local newspapers, Welsh mining villages and a little girl who put a penny in the Spitfire jar every time her family used the outdoor privy (she sent in a Postal Order for 15 shillings). The father of a dead RAF pilot donated £5,000 from his home village of Michaelston-le-Pit in Wales .*'I cannot provide you with another gallant son…the one who has gone was my only son,'* he wrote…

Money poured in from the great and the good. Queen Wilhelmina of the Netherlands, a country now under the Nazi boot, gave £500,000. The Nawab of Junagadh contributed £15,000. A gift of £30,000 came in from the New Zealand Meat Producers Board. The Kennel Club bought a Spitfire and called it *'The Dog Fighter.'* Countries made donations

large enough to sponsor an entire Squadron of Spitfires. 94 Squadron was sponsored by Trinidad and 114 Squadron by Hong Kong. A Spitfire emblazoned *'Dorothy of Great Britain and Empire'* was funded by girls named Dorothy. It was madness, but it was glorious madness from the finest hearts. Tongue firmly in cheek, an RAF pilot wrote to The Times complaining that there was not a Hurricane Fund. *'Perhaps the Spitfire has more sex appeal?'* he teased.

Ultimately, the Spitfire Fund raised some £13 million (around £670 million today). It would be churlish to disparage the heartfelt efforts that went into the Spitfire Fund. Cynics argue that Britain would build every Spitfire it wanted, entirely regardless of the little girl who believed in 'Spending a Penny' or a grieving Welsh father. The money raised, they say, was meaningless. That entirely misses the point. It was very meaningful indeed.

✈ BOTTOM: A shopper at London's Lambeth Walk's market contributes to the Spitfire fund

THE BATTLE OF BRITAIN

FLAMING JUNE

'The Battle of France is over. I expect that the Battle of Britain is about to begin.'

Winston Churchill, 18 June 1940

In June 1940, Britain braced for invasion and the Germans worked furiously to occupy new captured forward air bases in Northern France and Belgium, and to replenish the losses sustained during the Blitzkrieg. In England, Dowding tried to consolidate his forces and co-ordinate his defences.

Hitler was now in an even stranger than usual state of mind. He had won the blitzkrieg in record time and was thoroughly enjoying humiliating the French but when it came to committing to invasion of Britain, he flinched. For some reason, the thought of a seaborne invasion chilled him. *'I am a coward on water,'* he confessed. Instead, Hitler still thought he could reason with Britain. *'I'll come to an understanding with England,'* he had told Goering on 18 June.

Certain members of Churchill's War Cabinet had been amenable to any chance of peace with Germany ever since they had first met. Chamberlain thought a 'compromise' should be sought while Lord Halifax had secretly been discussing peace terms with the Italian ambassador. Churchill was of a different mind. *'My policy,'* he declared, *'is a policy of war.'*

IF HITLER WANTED BRITAIN, HE'D HAVE TO FIGHT FOR HER.

Neither the German navy nor the army were particularly enamoured of launching a seaborne invasion. It was Goering in his capacity as head of the Luftwaffe who — as usual — knew just what the Fuhrer wanted to hear from him. Relishing the chance to embarrass his rival armed forces, he told Hitler he had absolute confidence in his air force's ability to blow the RAF from the skies. It would take about four weeks, he boasted and — when it was complete — the British would sue for peace knowing they were defenceless. There might never be the need to launch an invasion. Goering's confidence was infectious. Hitler was sold.

DRAWING UP BATTLELINES

Goering's initial plan was to provoke RAF Fighter Command to come up and fight in large numbers — and to be destroyed quickly and decisively in a short series of massive air engagements. Luftflottes II and III, now stationed on captured airfields in occupied France and

Belgium, would lead the assault across the Channel and over Southern England, with Luftflotte V in Denmark and Norway providing further striking power across the North Sea. The Luftwaffe had at its disposal approximately 1,200 bombers, 280 dive bombers and 980 fighter aircraft.

Dowding had correctly guessed the Luftwaffe's plan of attack and had worked out a way to best face it. He now had his fifty-two squadrons of fighters, which included 19 Spitfire squadrons and 25 Hurricane Squadrons. The other eight squadrons were comprised of outdated Gloster Gladiators, Boulton-Paul Defiants and Bristol Blenheims. Numbers were very tight, even at fifty-two squadrons and not all squadrons were up to strength in either pilots or machines.

Dowding decided to use what was known as the Fabian System — only putting small numbers of aircraft into the air at any given time to meet the enemy, a tactic which avoided large scale actions but which would gradually wear down the Luftwaffe while conserving men and machines. Dowding understood that, if he could successfully hold out for just a few months, Britain would be saved by winter. No seaborne invasion could be launched so late in the year. It was a tactic that would increasingly bring him into conflict with the head of 12 Group (Central England), the well-connected Air Vice Marshal Trafford Leigh-Mallory and his favourite squadron

leader, Douglas Bader. Both Leigh-Mallory and Bader wanted to fight with 'Big Wings' — clusters of squadrons to hit the incoming Luftwaffe with full force.

THE MK.I & MK.II SPITFIRE

The Mk.I and Mk.II Spitfires were the aircraft which were to fight the Battle of Britain. The Mk.Is were built exclusively by the Supermarine plants in Southampton while the Mk.IIs came off the production line at Castle Bromwich and would not see active service before August 1940. Some 1,556 Spitfire Mk.Is were built.

Mk.IIs came complete with the new Merlin XII engine and a Rotol wide-bladed constant speed propeller, giving the Mk.II a small top speed advantage over the Mk.I as well as a better rate of climb.

Mk.Is were routinely replaced by Mk.IIs as and when possible, with priority being given to Spitfire Squadrons involved in the Battle of Britain. By April 1941, the Mk.II was standard in RAF Spitfire Squadrons, but it would start to be phased out itself over 1941 in favour of the Mk.V. A total of 921 Mk.IIs were built in all, the majority being IIAs armed with eight machine guns.

✦ L-R: Trafford Leigh-Mallory; Douglas Bader; Merlin XII engine

✦ Spitfire Mark 1A of No 19 Squadron, Royal Air Force being re-armed between sorties at Fowlmere, Cambridgeshire, September 1940

KANALKAMPF

The Battle of Britain 'officially' began on 10 July 1940 with what the Germans called Kanalkampf — war over the English Channel. Goering had numerous reasons to want to dominate the Channel. Britain depended for its very survival on supplies brought in by convoy. The Luftwaffe needed to gain clear aerial superiority over the Channel to allow its invasion barges to cross with some safety. More than anything, Goering was challenging Britain's pride as the (until now) undisputed master of the seas. Surely, he reasoned, the RAF would have to throw everything against him.

The first day proved a major shock to Goering. A force of 24 Do.17 bombers with a fighter escort fifty-strong went after a convoy codenamed 'Bread'. They were hit by Spitfires from 64 and 74 Squadrons, along with a number of Hurricanes. Two German bombers were shot down for the loss of one Hurricane, which collided with a bomber. The real shock was that ten of their Bf.109 escorts were also brought down, mostly by the Spitfires. The battle set the pattern for pretty much the rest of July. German bombers — in small or large numbers — would go after shipping in the Channel with or without fighter escorts. In turn, radar would guide relatively small RAF fighter formations against them. The first weeks of combat confused the Germans. They could not understand why the RAF was limiting its fighter response. The optimists among them believed that the RAF must be much weaker than anticipated. The pessimists decided to wait and see.

Ground staff refuelling a Supermarine Spitfire Mk IIA of No. 19 Squadron RAF at Fowlmere, near Duxford in Cambridgeshire, September 1940

Dowding was not happy with his 'fighter boys' flying and fighting over water. If forced to bail out or ditch, a pilot had little more than a one in five chance of surviving. He asked for convoys to be temporarily rerouted so as not to serve as targets which then had to be defended. Churchill personally refused his request, saying that it would amount to a loss of faith if British ships could not use British waters — but by the end of July, the war over the Channel had become so fierce and so much damage was being done to shipping that many convoys were indeed re-routed.

Even as British authorities struggled to maintain control of the Channel, the Germans were trying to come to terms with their combat losses, which were far higher than had been anticipated. By the end of Kanalkampf, 180 Luftwaffe planes had been lost to the RAF's seventy.

AUGUST 1940 – ADLERANGRIFF

By 8 August, Goering was still banking on a final great battle. He would launch the 'Attack of the Eagles' — Adlerangriff — which would start with an epic assault codenamed Adlertag (Eagle Day). It was time to hit radar facilities, airfields and aircraft production plants. The RAF simply could not afford to lose these. They would have to come up and fight to protect them. Goering now believed the RAF could be smashed in just four decisive days.

 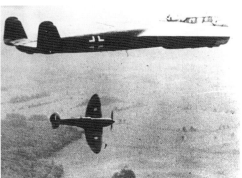 

Adlerangriff was planned to begin on 10 August but was postponed due to violent thunderstorms. On 11 August, the Luftwaffe launched the largest single air raid so far. The RAF fighters and the German fleet collided all along the Dorset coast between Weymouth and Swanage. It proved to be a brutal wake up call for both sides. By the end of the day, the Luftwaffe had lost 38 aircraft including 15 Bf.109s and 10 Bf.110s fighters. The RAF lost six Spitfires and 21 Hurricanes.

On 12 August, the Luftwaffe went after radar stations and airfields all over the south-east, often using Bf.109 and 110 fighters converted to carry a single bomb. Thirty-one of the raiders were brought down compared with Fighter Command losses of twenty-two. 13 August — the day designated as *Adlertag* — descended into chaos when the mass raids were called off due to bad weather — but no-one told the bombers, who then flew straight into the RAF fighters without the benefit of escorts. Confusion continued into the afternoon, and at the end of the day, RAF Spitfires and Hurricanes had brought down 47 enemy aircraft for the loss of just thirteen of their own.

Goering upped the ante. On 15 August, 800 Luftwaffe bombers escorted by 1,000 fighters took off for England, comprising the largest raid of the war so far. Once again, their targets were air bases and radar stations in South-East England. Fighter Command was stretched almost to breaking point to respond to such a large scale attack and had to call on reserves from all four Fighter Groups during the day. It was still not enough. Many of the raiders got through to their targets, causing severe damage. As night fell, the Germans tallied up their losses. They had lost seventy-five aircraft in a single day, compared with RAF losses of just thirty with 13 pilots killed. Churchill would call 15 August '*one of the greatest days in history.*' Henceforth, the Germans would refer to it as *der Schwarze Donnerstag* — Black Thursday.

Despite their formidable losses, the Luftwaffe returned in force the next day. West Malling aerodrome was knocked out. Stukas screamed down on Tangmere airfield, destroying 17 Spitfires on the ground as below them pilots raced to refuel and rearm. More Stukas swooped on Ventnor radar station, causing so much damage that the installation would be out of action for days. Prime Minister Winston Churchill personally followed the progress of the raids from 11 Group Headquarters at Uxbridge and saw for himself how stretched fighter defences had become. At one point in the day every single fighter squadron in the Group had been committed — and yet more German raiders

✈ L-R: German He-111 bombers on mission flight against England. above the french coast; Dornier Do 17 in combat with Supermarine Spitfire; Group of four Me 109s in line abreast

being called upon to fly four or even five separate combat missions over the course of a single day, racing home to refuel and rearm between sorties. Losses inevitably mounted during the day and finally stood at twenty fighters by the time Churchill left Uxbridge. He sat in his staff car, visibly shaken, and demanded silence from his Chief of Staff, General Hastings 'Pug' Ismay. Finally, he managed to sum up his feelings, saying *'Never in the field of human conflict has so much been owed by so many to so few'*.

Neither side could sustain this intense level of combat for much longer. The 'Few' were getting fewer — 78 RAF pilots had been killed in just eight days. On the other side of the Channel, the Luftwaffe had lost almost fifty aircraft over the course of that Friday alone. Saturday 17 August was quiet — so quiet that some radar operators were scared their systems had gone 'on the fritz'. RAF ground crews took the opportunity presented by the lull in the fighting to effect vital repairs on the airfields. Spitfire pilots rested on what one described as a 'heavenly day'. They read the papers, played a little football in the bright sunshine and celebrated just being alive in the pub come evening. It wasn't to last.

On Sunday 18 August the Luftwaffe came again — and in almost overwhelming force. By lunchtime, radar had picked up huge German formations assembling across the Channel. Every single Squadron in 11 Group was put on alert. Once again the Luftwaffe hit a succession of airfields and radar stations but once again the Spitfires and Hurricanes intercepting them extracted a high price — almost seventy enemy planes destroyed. The RAF for their part lost just over thirty planes in combat, not counting those destroyed on the ground. Only 10 pilots had been killed. Goering had wanted a decisive battle. What he was

getting instead was a gruelling, drawn-out war of attrition.

On the battered and cratered airfields now, the pilots were facing near-exhaustion. They could be called upon to fly possibly five combat sorties every single day — and flying seven sorties was far from unheard of. They had to be on call from 3am every single morning. The pilots of 32 Squadron at Biggin Hill took to sleeping out under the wings of their Hurricanes using their parachutes as pillows, while 151 Squadron pilots at Rochford started sleeping in the cockpits of their already fuelled up and armed fighters. One Spitfire pilot made a perfect landing at his home airfield — only to be discovered asleep at the stick.

ON 20 AUGUST, CHURCHILL WAS MOVED TO GIVE ONE OF HIS FINEST SPEECHES, PRAISING THE EFFORTS OF THE RAF:

'Never in the field of human conflict was so much owed by so many to so few. All hearts go out to the fighter pilots, whose brilliant actions we see with our own eyes day after day...'

It was not until Saturday 24 August that the Germans returned with any real force. Over the course of the day, they sent more than 500 aircraft over the Channel in six concerted waves. Spitfires and Hurricanes met them hard and a number of raids were turned back, but one raid saw ten German bombers lose their way and accidentally bomb London, starting fires from Bethnal Green to Oxford Street. Nine Londoners died. Bombing London was strictly forbidden by Hitler — but it was an accident just waiting to happen, and when it did it would have far-reaching consequences.

In the meantime, the massed German raids continued.

✈ L-R: Bf 110C of Zerstörergeschwader 76 over the English Channel; Messerschmitt Bf 110 from Zerstörergeschwader 26 (3U+DT) with two 900l drop tanks; View along the River Thames in London towards smoke rising from the London docks after an air raid during the Blitz.

✈ View of fire boats as they battle flames after a German air raid during the Battle of Britain, London, England, September 1940

Monday 26 August saw the Luftwaffe losing some 67 aircraft to the RAF's 27. Frustrated, Goering threw almost everything he had at South East England on Friday 30 August. Three giant waves of enemy aircraft swept in. The skies over South East England were packed with aircraft formations and wheeling dogfights. By noon everything 11 Group had was in the air. Three more waves of Luftwaffe fighters and bombers joined the melee in the early afternoon. Shoreham, Tangmere and Kenley airfields were all bombed by Ju.88s. Seven vital radar stations were knocked out. Between four and six pm nineteen more Luftwaffe Gruppren came over, looking for airfields and aircraft factories. The Vauxhall Works at Luton was badly damaged. Ju.88s caught 79 Squadron on the ground at Biggin Hill, destroying three Spitfires and obliterating one of the airfield's four remaining hangars.

The Luftwaffe started early on the morning of 31 August. A large formation of Luftwaffe bombers and Bf.110s split up over the Thames Estuary and struck RAF airfields including North Weald and Debden. Croydon and Biggin Hill were hit later in the day. Exhausted, Fighter Command struggled to cope with intercepting the enemy while their home airfields were being subject to attack — and the strain showed in the combat tally at the end of the day's fighting. The Luftwaffe still lost 39 aircraft — but the RAF had lost 37 of their own, with 13 pilots killed. The battle was now turning in favour of the Germans…

The large-scale air battles and constant pummelling of aerodromes of late August had left the RAF in a parlous state. New pilots — the sprogs- were proving no substitute for the veterans lost. They had a tendency to die quickly and pointlessly, fodder for more experienced adversaries. The Germans were suffering too. During July and August, the Luftwaffe had lost some 800 fighters and bombers.

However, the accidental bombing of civilian areas of London on the night of the 24/25 gave Winston Churchill all the justification he needed to lash out against Nazi Germany. On the night of 25/26 August, 95 Hampdens and Whitleys from RAF Bomber Command bombed Berlin in retaliatory raids. Few Berliners were killed in the raids and damage was only slight, but both Goering and Hitler were beside themselves with fury at the affront to the Reich. Goering was instructed to turn his attention away from the RAF's airfields — and to unleash the full might of the Luftwaffe against London instead.

CHANGING TACTICS

7 September was a beautiful sunny day. After a morning spent touring his airfields, Goering sat down on the cliffs of Cap Gris Nez overlooking the Channel and unpacked a large and lavish picnic. As he tucked in, he was quite convinced that today he would see the end of the RAF. By 4pm, a force of almost 1,000 Luftwaffe fighters and bombers were assembling in the air above — 348 bombers with 617 fighter escorts. It was the greatest flotilla the Luftwaffe had ever put into the air, a formation two miles high and spread across almost 800 square miles. Stunned by the radar signals and reports of 'many hundreds of aircraft' by the Observer Corps, the RAF initially threw up 11 squadrons and readied all the rest. 10 and 12 Group were put on standby.

It was a complete shock when bombs began falling on the city of London instead of the airfields. The Luftwaffe's initial bomb run was virtually unchallenged except for anti-aircraft fire from the London batteries — but then RAF squadrons began to arrive — 23 of them — diving on both the returning bomber formations and the new ones coming in. Bf.109 escorts slammed into them in turn. Those not in

✈ Huge area of debris in London after heavy German air raid bombing attacks during the Battle of Britain

shelters were treated to the sight of what was effectively a thousand aircraft dogfight high above their heads. The Bf.109s had to break off first as their fuel ran low and the bombers were left to fight their way home, harassed by the RAF fighters until their tanks too ran low.

As night fell over London, German raiders returned in waves that lasted until 5am the following morning, dropping more high explosives and more incendiaries into the fires already raging. 430 people died. 1600 were wounded. It was the first full day of 'the Blitz'. The next day, Park saw the devastation for himself as he flew over the stricken city in his personal Hurricane. He was horrified — but he also grasped right there and then that the Germans had made a potentially fatal tactical mistake. By switching their attention to London, they would be giving the RAF airfields a vital breathing space in which to sort themselves out.

The air defence of London had not gone well, however. Only 38 German fighters and bombers had been shot down and in doing so the RAF had lost 28 aircraft of its own. The bombers returned to London at 7.30pm on the 8th, as the RAF struggled to switch tactics and find how best to tackle the raiders. They coped well. The Luftwaffe returned on the 9th but most of the day's raids were driven off and 28 Luftwaffe aircraft downed at a cost of 21 RAF fighters.

Goering however was told that the RAF was on the verge of collapse. The fighting force, he believed, was down to its very last 50 Spitfires. He decided to test those reports on the first day with perfect weather. This turned out to be Sunday 15 September. At around 10.45am, radar reports started coming in of a large German force assembling over the Pas de Calais. It comprised a hundred Dorniers escorted by two hundred Bf.109 escorts. Park had no doubt the target was to be London, All 11 Group squadrons were

readied in a matter of minutes and 10 and 12 Group notified of the need to help. Spitfires of 72 and 92 Squadrons hit the Luftwaffe formation over Maidstone. The Bf.109s went after them, only to be bounced by 603 Squadron. More Bf.109s got sucked in to aid their fellow Messerschmitts, creating a hole through which 253 and 501 fighters managed to get at the Dorniers. More and more RAF squadrons piled into the epic aerial battle as the formation progressed over Kent, until the Germans found themselves under attack by 250 fighters from 23 different squadrons. A further six squadrons joined the fight as the bomber fleet reached the suburbs of south London, then five squadrons of the Duxford Wing of 12 Group came diving down on the Dorniers just as they were dropping their bombs. The bomber formations scattered, individual planes wheeling and accelerating everywhere in a desperate attempt to escape. Having broken formation, there was little their escorts could do to protect them. RAF fighters harassed them all the way south back over the Channel as well as up the length of the Thames into the North Sea.

As the RAF squadrons raced home to land, refuel and rearm, reports came in of another colossal German aerial armada sweeping in in three waves — a total of 150 bombers escorted this time by 400 fighters. They crossed the coast near Dungeness at 2.15pm, spread across ten full miles of sky. Spitfires from 41 and 603 Squadrons hit them over Romney Marshes. 73 Squadron were next, destroying three bombers off Maidstone. Spitfires from 66 and 72 Squadrons intercepted them over Dartford, quickly reinforced by four more squadrons. Hurricanes of 303 (Polish) hit bombers and their Bf.110 fighters over Gravesend. 213 and 607 Squadron Hurricanes punched into the bombers above the borders of Surrey. Wherever the bombers flew, they flew into more trouble.

The nerve of the Luftwaffe bomber pilots began to crack under the sheer weight of the assaults on them. The formations teetered. Some individual bombers broke formation and fled. Others dumped their bombs. Those who held their nerve faced a wall of flak from London's recently improved AA defences as they reached the outskirts of the city. After negotiating that, they suddenly found themselves facing 15 more squadrons of RAF fighters, comprising a Big Wing of five 12 Group Squadrons and ten 11 Group squadrons. It was a truly terrifying sight. The German bomber formations — suddenly faced with a sky full of fresh hostile fighters lost what was left of their discipline and their formations began to come apart. They dropped their bombs pretty much just anywhere and then tried to flee for home. They were harassed by fighters every single step of the way.

Over in France, the sight of one damaged bomber after another limping its way home and then spilling out wounded and dying air crew told its own story. The RAF were far from finished and something pretty much decisive had just happened. Back across the Channel, the RAF pilots and their commanders knew that too. There were reports of 183 German aircraft shot down. It wasn't true — the real number was fifty-six — but it felt to the fighter pilots as if they had decimated the Luftwaffe that day. RAF losses stood at just 26 — and a full half of the pilots shot down had survived.

On 17 September, Hitler finally lost faith in any and all invasion plans. The events of 15 September in the air over Britain had convinced him that the RAF were far from defeated. He ordered the invasion to be postponed indefinitely. It was a frank acknowledgement that Goering had failed to destroy the RAF and that bombing the capital would not lead to British pleas for surrender.

TARGET SUPERMARINE

Once the Germans had realised just how important the Spitfire was, it became vital to destroy the Spitfire factories. The first strike against Supermarine came in July 1940, when a formation of Heinkel 111s hit the nearby Cunliffe-Owen plant, but missed both the Supermarine flight shed (which was then jam-packed with Spitfires) and the Spitfire assembly sheds. Another raid on 15 September, this time by eighteen Me.110s carrying a bomb under each wing, only succeeded in blowing out some windows.

At 1.30pm on 24 September 1940, the Luftwaffe returned to the Spitfire plants, this time with much deadlier effect. Over fifty Bf.109s, equipped with bombs, swarmed and attacked. The Itchen Works were critically damaged and bombs scored direct hits on two air raid shelters. Ninety Supermarine

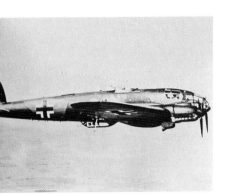

✈ L-R: Heinkel He 111; German Heinkel He 111s during the Battle of Britain; Heinkel He 111 bomber flying over Wapping and the Isle of Dogs in the East End of London

workers were killed and a further forty injured. The bombers returned on 26 September to finish the job. Seventy-six Heinkel 111s and Ju.88s, with a sixty strong Bf.110 fighter escort headed inwards with a purpose. Only nine Spitfires could be raised against them and they were simply brushed aside. Thirty-seven more employees died and Spitfire production in Southampton came to a complete halt.

Lord Beaverbrook was on the scene within a day of the raid. It was immediately obvious to him that the Supermarine plants could not be salvaged. Even as vital tools and jigs were being dug out of the ruined factories, Beaverbrook set to work dispersing Supermarine production to small and inconspicuous locations throughout the south of England, including Hampshire, Wiltshire, Dorset and Berkshire. More garages and car showrooms were requisitioned, along with laundries, bus depots, warehouses and even a strawberry-basket factory. Thirty five such sites were up and in production within just six weeks.

The dispersal scheme worked. After Supermarine Southampton was bombed out of its old works, it went on to build 8,000 more Spitfires across over 35 different dispersal sites with a workforce of some 10,000 civilians, almost half of them women.

THE DYING DAYS

With the invasion plan for England now on hold and the RAF increasingly successful at intercepting and disrupting bomber formations during the daylight hours, the Luftwaffe finally took the decision to end the practice of regular large scale bomber raids by conventional bombers over England in daylight. The end of October merely confirmed that the RAF were in charge now. The month had seen 379 Luftwaffe aircraft shot down for the loss of 185 RAF fighters. 31 October is officially regarded as the last day of the Battle of Britain.

The air battle had been very evenly matched. The RAF had lost 1,087 planes and 481 pilots. 357 Spitfires had been shot down, together with 601 Hurricanes. The Luftwaffe had lost 1,652 aircraft and just over 3,000 pilots and air crew. Of the aircraft lost 778 were bombers. 533 Bf.109s were shot down.

A GRAVE INJUSTICE

Almost as soon as the Battle of Britain was over, Air Chief Marshal Sir Hugh Dowding, Air Officer Commanding RAF Fighter Command was sacked from his post with what can only be described as indecent and spiteful haste. In

✈ Hawker Hurricane

 Air Chief Marshal Sir Trafford Leigh-Mallory

November of 1940, he was sacked by a single phone call and bluntly told *'The Air Council has no further work for you.'* He was given just twenty-four hours to clear his desk and go. Described as *'almost blind with fatigue'* from the effort of winning the Battle — and true to his own quiet nature — he made no protest and just went. Air Vice Marshal Keith Park — Commander of 11 Group and the man had had perhaps done more than any other to win the Battle of Britain — was also fired brutally and unceremoniously.

The reason given was that both men were essentially too defensive in their thinking, that they had disregarded the superior tactic of 'Big Wings' proposed by 12 Group Commander Leigh-Mallory, and that neither had any answer to the bombing of London by night. In truth, Leigh-Mallory had the ear of important figures in government and Dowding and Park did not. It was Leigh-Mallory who now was rewarded by being given the plum job of commander of 11 Group.

Across the Channel, Goering kept his job and desperately tried to salve his bruised ego. He began to let it be known that he wanted to be known by the nickname of 'Iron Man'. His pilots called him 'Fatty' instead.

SPITFIRE VERSUS HURRICANE

The Battle of Britain was barely over before analysts set about working out how the aircraft of Fighter Command had performed. What they really wanted to know was whether the Hurricane or the Spitfire had performed best against their Luftwaffe opposition. More Hurricanes had flown and fought in the battle than Spitfires — and the two aircraft were often deployed in quite different ways — but, allowing

for this, the maths quickly proved what everyone already knew. The Spitfire was clearly the better fighter plane. It was calculated that the average Spitfire survived combat for a third longer than a Hurricane. It was also noted that, for every 23 Luftwaffe aircraft accounted for by Hurricanes, Spitfires managed to bring down 27 despite often being vectored against fighters rather than bombers. On 14 October 1940, it was noted in an Air Staff meeting that *'… the Hurricane is found not a match for the Messerschmitt. The Spitfire retains its superiority.'* Production and development would now concentrate on the Spitfire.

THE LONG ROAD

LEAVING HOME

In the late winter of 1940-1941, the Luftwaffe came almost exclusively in darkness. The Spitfire was never a good night fighter. Cockpit visibility issues made it difficult to take off and land at night, it was harder to compensate for torque and the Spitfire's undercarriage was unforgiving of misjudgements. Beaufighters and Defiants with on-board radar became the RAF's primary night fighters. Spitfires largely sat on the airfields.

The Spitfire had only ever been designed for one purpose — to blow enemy bombers out of British skies. Now, with the threat of invasion over, it would have to adapt to fulfil other roles in a widening world and a widening war if it wanted to remain potent and useful. Some, like photoreconnaissance, it had already proven to perform quite exceptionally. However, what was now needed was a fighter capable of escorting bombers into enemy territory — and the Spitfire had a notoriously short range. As part of a strategy to bring the war to the enemy, the Spitfire would also need to perform a variety of ground attack roles — something R.J. Mitchell had never even envisioned.

These were all vital concerns for the war effort, but Joe Smith and his design team had even greater worries to contend with. German aviation technology was advancing rapidly, and the Spitfire would have to be evolved to meet — and hopefully exceed — the capabilities of a new generation of German fighters.

L-R: VIIA radar in Bristol Beaufighter; Boulton Paul Defiant; Bristol Beaufighter MAIN IMAGE: Boulton Paul Defiants of No. 264 Squadron RAF being prepared for take-off at Kirton-in-Lindsey, Lincolnshire

MARK III, IV AND MARK V

✈ ───────────────────

Long before the Battle of Britain had even begun, Joe Smith and his team were already at work on a new kind of Spitfire. The Spitfire Mk III would take advantage of Rolls-Royce's latest Merlin XX engine, supplying an extra 215hp over the present Merlin XII. Crucially, the Spitfire Mk.III would be noticeably faster than its predecessors (and its rivals), perhaps even capable of 400mph. The prototype first flew in March 1940 and an order for 1,000 aircraft was placed, with delivery due to start in early 1941. Unfortunately for the Mk.III, Hurricanes were already being promised the Merlin XX to stop them becoming obsolete and Supermarine had to abandon the Mk.III.

Much was expected of the new Spitfire Mk. IV, intended to be available to squadrons by August 1941. It would be powered by a new 37-litre Rolls-Royce Griffon engine, increasing its speed to 420mph as well as boosting its climb performance. Designers talked excitedly about equipping it with six 20mm cannon or even a dozen Brownings. However, by the time the first Mk.IV flew in late November 1941, it had already been superseded by the Mk.V. The Mk.IV had only been intended to be a stop-gap measure until the Mk.V came along, but the appearance of the new and deadlier Messerschmitt BF.109F panicked everyone into committing fully to the Mk.V. More Mk.V Spitfires would be produced than any other mark — 6,787 in all. Fitted with a new and improved Merlin 45 engine, the Spitfire V now had a top speed of 369 mph at 18,500ft and improved climbing and manoeuvring abilities, allowing it to match the Bf.109F more closely in combat.

There were to be two main versions of the MK.V. First came the VA armed with eight Browning machine gun, but just 94 were built before production switched to the VB which was packed with two cannon and four Brownings to give it more destructive firepower. A third version, the VC had a 'universal wing' which could be adapted to different cannon and machine gun configurations, depending on operational requirements. By the end of 1941, 44 RAF squadrons had been upgraded to the new Mk V.

LOOKING FOR TROUBLE - RHUBARBS, CIRCUSES, RAMRODS & ROADSTEADS

✈ ───────────────────

Through the winter of 1940 and the spring of 1941, the Luftwaffe came almost exclusively by night. Hundreds of Spitfires sat idly on the English airfields, their pilots bored and restless. More and more Spitfires were being produced,

✠ L-R: Spitfire PR Mark IVs; Supermarine Spitfire Mark V; American volunteer pilots of No.121 (Eagle) Squadron run to their Mark V at RAF Rochford

but the fighting capability they offered went unused.

As the year turned, the new AOC of Fighter Command, Temporary Air Marshal Sholto Douglas, decided to give his pilots something to do — just to keep them mean and keen. Naturally inclined to the offensive, unlike his predecessor Dowding, Douglas (together with the Head of 11 Group, Leigh-Mallory) came up with a number of different offensive missions that could be flown over Northern France, Holland and Belgium. *'Last year our fighting was desperate but now we are entitled to be more cocky,'* wrote Leigh-Mallory.

By January 1941, Fighter Command had stolen the German idea of 'bombers as bait' and were sending a single bomber unit over to occupied France — with up to five Spitfire squadrons ready to pounce on the Luftwaffe as they flew to intercept. They called these operations 'Circuses'. Shortly after, Fighter Command started operating mass fighter sweeps across Europe known as 'Rhubarbs' intended to provoke a German fighter response and low level strikes against German shipping referred to as 'Roadsteads'. Hurribombers distinguished themselves on 'Ramrod' raids, flying short-range bombing operations against targets such as harbours and airfields.

✈ L-R: A formation of five Blenheim Mark IVs ; Arming a Focke-Wulf Fw 190 fighter plane with 21 launchers in the hangar; Focke-Wulf Fw 190A

✠ Air Marshall W Sholto Douglas

While the missions boosted public morale, and kept the pilots busy, in terms of war aims, they achieved very little. Spitfires drank petrol and were not suited to longer missions ranging over Europe. Spitfire pilots began to hate flying at slow speeds so that the Blenheims could keep up with them, and quite naturally the bomber crews didn't appreciate being used as bait. Nevertheless, these missions were to

continue, on and off, until D-Day three years hence.

Even with new Mk.Vs, dogfighting with the latest Me.109Fs proved gruelling and low level flying left the Spitfires vulnerable to even relatively light anti-aircraft fire. As a result, casualties on the RAF's part were high. Pilots shot down over enemy territory were almost certain to be taken prisoner, unlike when they had fought over English soil. Across the summer of 1941, RAF Fighter Command lost over 200 pilots on such raids, including legendary Battle of Britain fighter aces like Eric Lock, shot down by ground fire and killed and even Wing Commander Douglas Bader, who was brought down and taken prisoner. The following year, such missions claimed the life of Air Commodore Paddy Finucane, while Wing Commander Robert Stanford Tuck was shot down and captured. *'Bloody murder,'* was how ace Johnnie Johnson came to describe Rhubarb raids — *'I loathed those Rhubarbs with a deep, dark hatred.'*

FOR THOSE SPITFIRE PILOTS ENGAGED IN RHUBARBS AND CIRCUSES, THINGS WERE ABOUT TO GET EVEN WORSE.

In late 1941, RAF pilots over Europe began to report seeing a new German fighter, with markedly better fighting characteristics than either the Me.109 or the Spitfire. RAF pilots commonly referred to this new and lethal German fighter as a 'brute' and losses against it very swiftly mounted . It seemed to all as if it could chew even a new Spitfire V to bits without hardly trying. The Focke-Wulf 190 had arrived.

THE MARK IX SPITFIRE

When Dowding fully understood what was happening in the dogfights between Spitfires and the new Fw.190s, he fired off a letter to Winston Churchill declaring that the Spitfire was dead. The Fw.190 had it totally outclassed in both performance and 'hitting power'. Dowding could not imagine the Spitfire rising to this challenge. *'One may conjure a quart out of a pint pot but one can't get a gallon, '* he warned.

What he didn't know was that Joe Smith's team were working flat out to prove him wrong. The Spitfire could and would be improved further still. At first, the answer to the Fw.190 threat seemed to be the Spitfire VIII, which featured the new Merlin 61 engine with a two-stage supercharger. Initial tests were very promising, but to accommodate the new engine the Spitfire's airframe would require extensive modification — and

that would take precious time. The VIII would fly and fight eventually (mostly in the Mediterranean and the Far East) — but something was needed much sooner.

Supermarine raced to find a way to retrofit a Merlin 61 engine onto a Spitfire Mk.IX with as little trouble and rejigging as possible. It worked. The new Mk.IX could now do 409 mph at 28,000 feet. It enjoyed a service ceiling of 43,000 feet — an improvement of around 7,000 feet — and it could climb at 4,000 feet a minute. Test-flown against a captured Fw 190, it appeared to be very evenly matched.

Full production of the Spitfire Mk.IX began in June 1942 and within a month the first IXs were flying with 64 Squadron out of Hornchurch. On 30 July 1942, the Spitfire IX shot down five Fw.190s in a single day, the very first kill being credited to Flight Lieutenant Donald E. Kingaby DFC from 64 Squadron who recorded in his Combat Report:

'We sighted approx. 12 Fw.190s two thousand feet below us at 19,000 ft just off Boulogne proceeding towards French coast. We dived down on them and I attacked a Fw.190 from astern and below giving a very short burst, about ½ sec. from 300 yds. I was forced to break away as I was crowded out by other Spits. I broke down and right and caught another Fw as he commenced to dive away. At 14,000 ft. approx. I gave a burst of cannon and M/G, 400 yds range, hitting E/A along fuselage. Pieces fell off and E/A continued in straight dive nearly vertical. I followed E/A down to 5,000 ft. over Boulogne and saw him hit the deck just outside of Boulogne and explode and burn up. Returned to base at 0 ft.'

Three main versions of the Mk.IX were produced. The original, powered by the Merlin 61, was designated F.Mk.IX and 1,255 were built. This was followed in early 1943 by the Merlin 63 or 66-powered IX designated LF Mk.IX, which was so successful that a total of 4010 came off the production line. Around 10% of the IXs were built by Supermarine in the south but the vast majority were produced at Castle Bromwich. Over fifty RAF and Commonwealth squadrons would be equipped with Spitfire IXs.

DIEPPE

On 19 August 1942, a large-scale Allied amphibious raid was launched on the small French port of Dieppe. The action was taken for a number of reasons: to appease Stalin's insistence on more action being taken in the West; to raise public morale at home and to gain useful

✛ L-R: Spitfire Mark IX of No 64 Squadron, undergoing an engine overhaul; Machinegun position, Dieppe; Churchill tank at Dieppe raid

✛ Spitfire Mk IXE, armed with a 250-lb GP bomb under each wing

information on how to conduct beach assaults.

At 05.00 hours, 6,000 Canadian and British troops stormed ashore from landing craft, supported by over fifty Churchill tanks. By the time the order to withdraw was given, just a few hours later, almost half had been killed or taken prisoner.

RAF commanders had looked forward to their part in the operation with some relish. Like their German counterparts during the Battle of Britain, the RAF hoped to lure the Luftwaffe into committing to a massed battle in which significant numbers of the enemy could be destroyed. Command of the Allied air operations supporting the raid was given to Air Vice Marshal Leigh-Mallory, who deployed 48 Spitfire squadrons in support of the operation. What he completely failed to appreciate was that the vast majority of them were still flying the old Spitfire Mk.V — and the

✝ Josef Wurmheller

⊬ Poster depicts a Churchill Infantry tank disembarking from a landing craft

opposition would comprise a substantial number of Fw 190s…

Predictably, the Fw.190 took a hellish toll on Allied aircraft over the port. Oblt. Sepp Wurmheller of JG 2, for example, despite having a broken leg in plaster and having been shot down early in the morning, took up another Fw.190 and alone succeeded in shooting down no less than seven Spitfires and a Blenheim bomber.

In what proved to be the largest single day air battle of all time, Fighter Command lost 91 aircraft, of which 62 were Spitfires and the RCAF lost a further 14 planes. An additional six Allied bombers were destroyed. By comparison, Luftwaffe losses were just 48 aircraft. The RAF had failed to win any sort of decisive victory and the Luftwaffe components in the region were back up to full

tank landing craft lead our attack

OUR ENGINES POWER THE OFFENSIVE

strength again within just a few days. When he first heard the casualty figures, Leigh-Mallory refused to believe them, claiming it was all a Luftwaffe trick.

SPITFIRES OVER MALTA

When the first Spitfires touched down on the Mediterranean island of Malta on 7 April 1942, they landed amidst the thick smoke of battle. The tiny island — smaller than the Isle of Wight — had been under attack almost since the day Mussolini had declared war on Britain in June 1940. Two years later, it had had earned the unenviable record of being the most bombed place on earth. Much of its population had taken to living in caves, abandoning the port towns and cities which were being struck from the air by day and night. Worse, supplies of virtually everything were running out as convoys desperately trying to resupply the island were mercilessly ravaged by Axis aircraft and sea power.

Just fifty miles south of Sicily, Malta stood squarely in the middle of the Axis shipping lanes supplying Italian and German forces in the battle for control of North Africa. Allied aircraft and shipping using Malta could dictate the possible outcome not just of the war in the Mediterranean, but of the campaigns in North Africa. By 1942 it was obvious that the

war in the Western Desert had reached a critical stage and the Axis air forces were making every effort to smash what resistance remained on Malta as a prelude to invasion. By March 1942, it is estimated that the Luftwaffe had almost 5,000 fighters and bombers ranged against Malta. Between 1 January and 24 July, there was just one solitary day when the island was not bombed.

In its defence, Malta had just a small shield of Hurricanes and, by February 1942, only 28 of these remained. They proved a poor match for the Bf.109F. Hurricane pilots were complaining bitterly that Luftwaffe fighter pilots were taunting them by deliberately flying right into their gunsights — before effortlessly outmanoeuvring the Hurricanes and escaping again.

Air Commodore Hugh Lloyd, the local RAF commander, began to beg for Spitfires to replace his aging Hurricanes. Government listened and, on 7 April 1942, the first Spitfires began to arrive on the island as part of Operation Spotter. Sixteen Tropicalized Spitfire VBs were shipped out from Gibraltar on board the aircraft carrier *HMS Eagle* and then, off the coast of Algiers, took off from the carrier to fly some 660 miles into Malta with the aid of special 90 gallon 'Slipper' drop tanks. This was the first overseas deployment for a Spitfire fighter squadron. This was also the first time

L-R: USS Wasp; Air Vice Marshal Keith Park about to taxi out in his personal Supermarine Spitfire V to mark the opening of Malta's new airstrip at Safi; Assembling Hawker Hurricane and Supermarine Spitfire in front of the Rock of Gibraltar

Spitfires had ever flown off a carrier but every one which took off made it to the island. They were needed for action almost immediately — but the numbers were still proving too few. For one five day period in early April, only one Spitfire on the island was airworthy. For two days not a solitary Spitfire could fly. The RAF were reduced to putting out fake radio signals to Spitfire squadrons that didn't exist in an effort to frighten the incoming bombers. On one occasion, the fake broadcasts so confused two German fighter pilots that they attacked and shot each other down. But the chicanery couldn't last for long.

In a desperate effort to get more Spitfires onto the island, Churchill asked Roosevelt to lend him the U.S. carrier Wasp to fly in a larger Spitfire force. Roosevelt agreed and on 13 April 47 Spitfires were packed aboard the carrier in Scotland and despatched on 20 April. They too were quickly swallowed up. The fight for Malta was now so intense that, within just three days, the majority of the Spitfire force was gone — eight shot down in dogfights, while a further 35 were destroyed or damaged on the ground by air raids. The Allies simply accepted the losses. Malta had to be saved.

Still more Spitfires flew out to Malta in a joint effort between the carriers Wasp and Eagle, flown by more combat-experienced pilots. Now up to 64 Spitfires could be sent to Malta in a single mission and Spitfires started to gain a precious foothold on the island. On what became known as 'The Glorious 10th of May', a total of 63 enemy aircraft were destroyed or damaged — 57 were credited to the RAF Spitfires and six others to anti-aircraft fire.

In July of 1942, the air defence of Malta passed into the hands of Keith Park, who used many of the tactics he had employed during the Battle of Britain to best effect. Now, Spitfires would intercept the Axis bomber formations out at sea on their way in, rather than chasing them after they had done their damage. The new tactic had a profound impact. The Axis stopped all daylight raids within just six days and withdrew all Stuka units from the fray, as they proved particularly vulnerable in combat with Spitfires. Not content with just defending Malta, Park's Spitfires would strike north and actually attack the raider's bases in southern Sicily. Spitfire VCs were adapted to carry 250lb bombs under each wing, acting as improvised dive bombers. By September 1942 the Spitfires of Malta, now numbering some 20 squadrons, had achieved air superiority and were even able to offer decisive protection to the Allied convoys. Vital supplies started arriving in bulk for the first time — including food, beer and aviation fuel.

Park kept up a good relationship with his pilots, touring the airfields in an MG or on a bicycle if fuel was particularly scarce. Morale grew fast — many of the veteran pilots had served under Park during the Battle of Britain — and Malta became known as 'the fighter pilot's paradise' amongst pilots. Here, far away from home, they could live wild and fight hard. The sky was filled with dogfights and the opportunities for kills plentiful.

The Germans came again in October, fearful that forces

⊬ Air Officer Commanding Malta, Air Vice Marshal Sir Keith Park, in the cockpit of his personal Supermarine Spitfire V before his ceremonial take-off at Malta's new aerodrome at Safi, May 1943

on Malta could wreck Rommel's campaign just before the crucial battle of El Alamein. On 10 October, five massed waves of German bombers swept in from the north but were intercepted by Spitfires and the Luftwaffe failed to drop a single bomb on the island. On the 15th Malta's air defences were judged so ferocious that a bombing force of just 14 aircraft was given a 98 plane fighter escort. On the 19th, the Luftwaffe tried again with 250 bombers and fighters, but the Spitfires shot down 46 of them. A month later, Axis attacks on the island started to peter out, as it became increasingly obvious that Malta would not fall. In total, the Axis lost some 350 aircraft in just over a month. In that time, a further 385 Spitfires had been flown into Malta, some later VC marks flying in directly all the way from Gibraltar — a flight of 1,100 miles — with massive 170 gallon drop tanks. 148 Spitfires were lost to aerial combat over Malta.

THE SEAFIRE

Such was the excitement generated by the Spitfire in 1938 that the Admiralty started to consider the Spitfire for carrier-based operations. By the end of 1939 Joe Smith had already attached an experimental arrestor hook to a Spitfire and flown the aircraft as the Type 338. Plans for folding wings were drawn up and it was planned to buy 50 such Spitfires for the FAA, to be delivered in July 1940 — but the demand for Spitfires during the Battle of Britain put all Fleet Air Arm claims on the Spitfire on hold.

By late 1941 the Admiralty again looked to the possibility of using Spitfires on carriers, the Hurricane having already been successfully converted. 48 Spitfire Mk.VBs were purchased by the Navy for experimental purposes, now fitted with arrestor hooks, and began flying from carriers as the Seafire Mk Ib. The results were not promising. The new Seafire could take off from carriers with no problems and could fight better than anything else the Navy had, but deck landings produced stresses on the fuselage that the Spitfire was never designed to cope with, leading to increased fatigue at best and a write off at worst. Fatigue also shortened the Merlin's engine life. And to top it all, the Seafire's landing gear proved to be inadequate to the task and liable to collapse. Indeed, far more Seafires were to

✠ Seafire being brought up onto the flight deck of HMS Furious

be lost to landing gear failure than to enemy action. Some hasty workarounds were produced and another 115 Spitfire Mk.VBs purchased for conversion. The first available models were supplied to 807 Squadron in June 1942. The Seafire Mk.IIC — considered by many to be the first 'real' Seafire — followed in September 1942. Supermarine built 262 Seafire IICs. Westland built a further 110. Despite 40,000 man hours being devoted to the IIC to get it properly ready for naval use, folding wings were not fitted until the arrival of the IIIC, which also included as standard the new and more powerful Merlin 55 engine. The Seafire IIIC was the variant built in the greatest numbers. A total of 1,220 were manufactured in all, the majority built by Westland while Cunliffe Owen produced 350 aircraft.

Seafires first saw combat in November 1942, flying as part of Operation Torch — the Allied invasion of North Africa — in American markings. In July 1943, they fought as part of Operation Husky — the Invasion of Sicily — and then in September 1943 as the invasion of Italy got underway.

106 Seafires from eleven squadrons were assigned aboard Royal Navy escort carriers to provide continuous air cover to the landings at Salerno in Italy, in September 1943 and while they proved successful in keeping Bf.109s and Fw.190s at bay, by D-Day +2, only 39 were still serviceable to fly. Ironically, the problem was that the sea was virtually like a millpond with

no wind to speak of. This meant that the carriers could not be sailed into a headwind, which could then be used to slow down the Seafires as they came in. As a result, many touched down too fast, missed the arrestor cables entirely and smashed into the crash barriers. It was a classic example of how the Seafire was an aircraft full of uncomfortable compromises, based on an aircraft never designed to serve at sea.

The RAF 'borrowed' a number of FAA Seafire squadrons for reconnaissance and target-spotting roles on D-Day in June 1944 and returned them a month later. In August 1944, Seafires stationed in the Mediterranean also saw action from four carriers as part of Operation Dragoon — the invasion of Southern France.

In late 1944, production switched to the Seafire FMk.XV with a Griffon VI engine. Supermarine built the first six prototypes, after which production switched once more to Westland and Cunliffe Owen who produced a total production run of 390 fighters. The extra power afforded by the new Griffon engine led to some unexpected technical problems, especially when manoeuvring on the deck of a carrier and this was finally addressed with the introduction of the Mk.XVII which boasted a strengthened undercarriage as well as reinforced wings and extra fuel tanks. 232 Mk XVII's were built, as usual divided between Westland and Cunliffe Owen.

✈ L-R: Fireflies, Barracudas, and Seafires (880 Squadron) on the deck of HMS Implacable; Seafire Mk IIc of No. 885 Naval Air Squadron on the flight deck of HMS Formidable in the Mediterranean, 1942; Fleet Air Arm Trials, Aboard HMS Victorious

Late 1944 also saw the Seafire taking part in operations against the Japanese in the Far East, acquitting itself well against its chief rival the Zero. Because of its limited range (which sometimes had to be boosted by borrowing American drop tanks) and its relatively light ordnance carrying capability, the Seafire was often used for Combat Air Patrol over the fleet rather than offensive missions. In this role it saw heavy combat against the waves of kamikazes menacing Allied ships off Okinawa. Carrier-based Seafires continued to fly against the Japanese right up to the cessation of hostilities. On 15 August 1945, Seafires took part in what is considered the very last dogfight of World War Two. Eight Seafire Mk.IIIs from 887 and 894 Squadrons took on twelve Japanese aircraft — eight A6M Zeros and four Mitsubishi J2M Raidens — above Tokyo Bay. One Seafire was shot down but seven enemy Zeros were accounted for.

Shortly after, fifty Seafire Mk.45s were built by Castle Bromwich. The first models — equipped with Griffon 60 series engines — entered service with 778 Squadron in November 1946, but were soon followed by the Seafire Mk.46 which would benefit from Griffon 85 or 87 engines powering two-three bladed Rotol contra-rotating propellers, a larger fuel capacity and bigger tail units to help offset the sheer power of the Griffon during deck manoeuvres. The last version of the Seafire to be produced, the Mk.47, is generally regarded as the finest. It had hydraulically-operated folding wings and Rotol contra-rotating propellers and would see action in both Malaya and Korea before being retired from front-line service in 1950. Ninety Mk.47s were built in all, the complete run coming from Supermarine.

SPITFIRES OVER NORTH AFRICA

Spitfires arrived in North Africa in relatively limited numbers in the spring of 1942 and almost immediately found

themselves caught up in 'Operation Theseus', as Axis forces surged east in a fresh offensive. Spitfires flew largely defensive patrols, provided top cover for Hurricanes on ground attack missions and went after the formations of bombers providing Rommel with close air support, but were progressively forced out of their forward landing strips and back across the desert. The Luftwaffe inflicted heavy losses on the Allies — 202 fighters in just six weeks — but were still not able to win aerial superiority. To an enemy used to battling 'inferior' fighters like the P-40 and Hurricane, the arrival of the Spitfire — even in very limited numbers — came as an unpleasant shock.

The Allied retreat finally came to a halt at the Alamein line at the end of July 1942 and held. The Spitfires of 145 and 601 Squadrons were in daily combat with the Luftwaffe, and flew as many as eight escort missions a day for fighter-bombers and bombers striking at Rommel's forces, forward air fields and critical supply lines. Other Spitfires especially

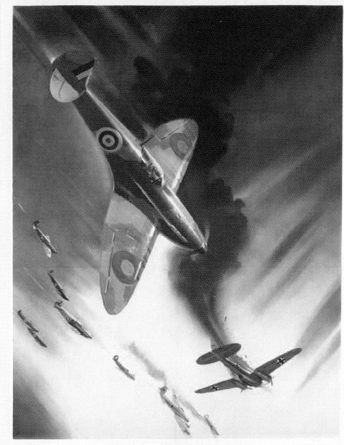

LIBYA
Help them finish the job

✈ Poster supporting the Libyian campaign

✈ The Royal Canadian Air Force In Tunisia, April 1943, Supermarine Spitfire Mk Vbs of No 417 Squadron, Royal Canadian Air Force flying in loose formation over the Tunisian desert providing cover for Allied bombers, April 1943

✠ The South African Air Force In Tunisia, April 1943, The Supermarine Spitfire pilot of ER622, No 40 Squadron, South African Air Force confers with his 'No 2' after landing at Gabes, April 1943

modified for high altitude interceptions went up against Ju.86 reconnaissance flights. On 1 August, 92 Squadron started re-equipping with Spitfires from Hurricanes to become only the third Spitfire squadron in North Africa.

In October 1942, the Allied counter-offensive began. Spitfires provided air cover and flew as escorts for bomber forces. Losses on both sides were heavy, but the Allied air assaults proved key in preventing German armour from concentrating successfully as well as disrupting vital supply lines. At the beginning of November, Axis forces began a headlong retreat westwards. They were harried from the air all the way, with the Spitfire squadrons now taking up residence on recaptured landing strips in Libya. In November 1942, No 1 Squadron of the South African Air Force also received their first Spitfires. A month later, Spitfires arrived for the Royal Canadian Air Force's 417 Squadron.

During November 1942, 118 Gibraltar-based Spitfires joined six squadrons of FAA Seafires in providing air support for Operation Torch — the landings in Morocco and Algeria. Spitfires also flew with the 31st and 52nd Fighter

Groups with the US 12th Air Force. After the Vichy French command surrendered, six Spitfire squadrons were based in Algeria, with more and more Mk.IX's being provided in the early months of 1943 to counter the threat of Luftwaffe Fw.190s now appearing in theatre.

By the start of 1943, Rommel's forces had retreated all the way back to Tunisia and were vulnerable to air attack from both Algeria to the west and the advancing Allied forces to the East. They held on the Mareth Line for three months, during which time the Spitfire Squadrons of 244 Wing gradually began to be supplied with Mk.IX's to replace their Mk.Vs. Other Mk.IX-equipped units flew in to join them, including formidable volunteer Polish fighter pilots attached to 145 Squadron and known collectively as the 'Polish Combat Team' who racked up a formidable number of kills in just a few months. Bf.109 pilots found the IX a very different proposition to fighting the old Spitfire Mk.V. A 'Spitfire Complex' quickly developed among them and they began to avoid battle if they could. As Squadron Leader Neville Duke observed '...the advent of the Mark IX was a revelation and a source of great joy.' In early May 1943,

✛ Collaboration Between Royal Air Force Spitfires and the Eighth Army during the Tunisian Campaign, Spring 1943

surviving Luftwaffe fighters were evacuated to Sicily — the Bf.109s flying with up to three ground crew hidden away in the fuselage and a further man sitting on the pilot's lap. It was a humiliating way to leave a war they had felt certain of winning just a year earlier.

Despite the Luftwaffe having deployed more aircraft to the war in Tunisia than they had to the Western Desert offensive — and despite the arrival of the formidable Fw.190 — by May 1943, Axis forces in Tunisia had been degraded and squeezed so hard that they elected to surrender.

AGAINST THE RISING SUN

By late 1942, the Japanese were battling to take control of New Guinea, and sending naval bomber forces to attack Darwin and other targets in North-West Australia. The Americans had supplied P-40s to help Australia defend the Northern Territories, but what the Australian government really wanted was Spitfires and appealed directly to Britain to get some. Churchill agreed and Spitfire squadrons were duly despatched in secrecy.

RAAF No1 Wing was formed flying Spitfire Mk .VCs and comprising two RAAF squadrons as well as RAF 54 Squadron. One of the RAAF Squadrons — 452 — had been formed in Britain in April 1941 and swiftly became one of the top scoring squadrons of that year under the command of Squadron Leader Ray 'Throttle' Thorold-Smith, himself an ace credited with eight kills. Now it had returned home to defend Australia. The second RAAF squadron returning home — 457 — had been stationed on the Isle of Man and had consequently seen much less action. Each squadron brought with it 16 Spitfires.

1 Wing scored its first kill — a Japanese 'Dinah' reconnaissance aircraft — on 2 February 1943. Flying out of Darwin, they were in heavy combat for most of 1943 and did not fare well. The Spitfire's limited range once again worked against it, even with extra tanks, as much of the combat took place a distance out to sea. The Japanese Zero also turned out to be a much tougher foe than anticipated, even able to out-turn even the Spitfire during dogfights. For its part the Spitfire was faster — and less likely to catch fire or explode when hit with just a relatively few shells. In the end, it was heavy Japanese losses elsewhere rather than I Wing that saw a significant reduction of Japanese raids on North Australia. From October 1943, a total of 410 Spitfire VIII's

 L-R: Japanese Navy Mitsubishi A6M5 "Zero" fighter in flight; Mitsubishi A6M Zero, 1942; Kiriwina, Trobriand Islands, Papua. November 1943, Supermarine Spitfire Mk Vc

were brought in to replace the VCs.

In November 1943, Spitfire VCs started reaching three squadrons stationed on the border of India and Burma. On Boxing Day 1943, two of these Spitfires tangled with a formation of Japanese bombers and their fighter escorts over Chittagong, bringing down three of the bombers and an escort. On New Year's Eve, Spitfires achieved an even better result, shooting down eleven Japanese bombers and three escorts. Mk.VIIIs began to replace the VCs starting from February 1944, just in time to play a major role in breaking the Japanese Ha-Go offensive, which had been launched to destroy isolated Indian divisions in Burma's Arakan province. The besieged Allied divisions desperately needed resupply by air, but transports were being beaten back by massed Japanese fighters. Three squadrons of Spitfires were targeted against them out of Chittagong and finally gained air superiority after days of near continuous

fighting which saw 65 Japanese aircraft destroyed for the loss of three Spitfires. The supplies began to get through and the Japanese ground offensive collapsed.

The next major challenge came in early 1944 when the Japanese attempted to break through into India. The strongest points of Allied ground resistance, around Kohima and Imphal, were stoutly defended by Spitfires and resupplied by Allied transports, for several months, until once again, the Japanese offensive broke. The Spitfires had helped to achieve air superiority over the besieged Allied strongpoints and maintained it afterwards, blitzing the Japanese ground formations as they fell back in some disarray. Spitfires played an important role as the Allies reconquered Burma, and launched devastating ground attacks with 500lb bombs during the mopping up operations against the last significant Japanese troop concentrations at the Sittang Bend in July and August of 1945.

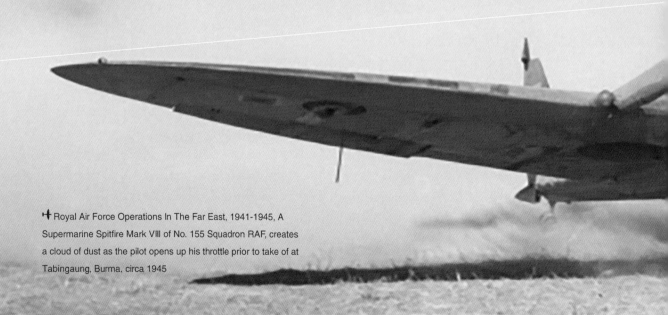

⊹ Royal Air Force Operations In The Far East, 1941-1945, A Supermarine Spitfire Mark VIII of No. 155 Squadron RAF, creates a cloud of dust as the pilot opens up his throttle prior to take of at Tabingaung, Burma, circa 1945

RED STAR SPITFIRES

In 1941, Britain shipped 200 Hurricanes to Russia to help the Soviet Union's war effort. Stalin dismissed them as 'shit'. After RAF Spitfire Mk.IV photoreconnaissance aircraft were sent to Russia in 1942 to help protect Soviet shipping, Stalin decided that what he really wanted was some Spitfires and duly requested them. Churchill readily agreed and got personally involved. Stalin was promised 150 reconditioned Mk.VBs, together with another 50 in spares 'as soon as possible'. These were handed over to the Soviet Air Force between January and March 1943. Soviet Spitfires first saw action on 28 April 1943 in the Kuban, attacking a formation of twelve Stukas, only to be bounced by their Bf.109 escorts. The Luftwaffe pilots were stunned to encounter Spitfires over the Eastern Front as were six Soviet Yak 1s who came to help. The Yaks ended up firing on their own Spitfires, while the Soviet Spitfires

also lost their leader in combat with a Bf.109 before the melee broke up. The Soviets immediately realised that they had an aircraft recognition problem on their hands, while the Luftwaffe pilots involved were told to keep silent about Spitfires in the hands of the Russians.

By the end of June 1943, the Soviet Squadrons flying Spitfires decided they didn't really like them and were re-equipped with patriotic Soviet-made aircraft. The Mk.V was not a good match against the Bf109G then appearing over the Soviet Union. By the time the IX came along in 1944, Spitfires were mainly relegated to serving with PVO air defence units in the rear, where the IX's relatively better high altitude performance was an advantage.

Despite this, Russia continued to demand Spitfires from Britain right up until the end of the war. 1,331 were delivered to the Soviet Union in all, the vast majority being Mk.IXs.

DESIGNED
FOR VICTORY

THE SPITEFUL AND THE SEAFANG

By late 1942, even Joe Smith and his design team started to wonder if the days of the Spitfire might be numbered. The war in the air was requiring fighters to be capable of faster and faster speeds and the Spitfire's elliptical wing design in particular, once such an asset, was now impeding its ability to fly still faster and higher. The solution, they decided would be a new, completely redesigned laminar flow wing.

The Air Ministry were impressed by the proposal and issued Specification F.1/43 in February 1943 to allow tests to proceed. As seems almost traditional with Spitfire-based designs, designing and building the new wing resulted in severe delays. The first prototype of what was then designated the Type 371, NN660, was flown by Jeffrey Quill on 30 June 1944, with the radical new wing mounted on a Spitfire XIV. Results were mixed. Three months later, NN660 crashed for reasons never fully understood, killing its test pilot Frank Furlong.

Supermarine pressed on, now making some substantial changes to the Spitfire fuselage to correct instability issues associated with the new Spitfire Griffon engine. The finished

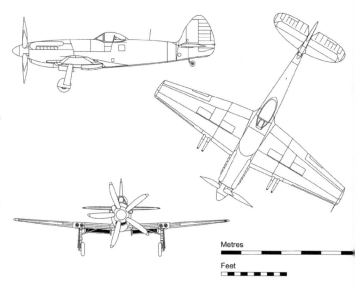

Metres

Feet

design was substantially different to the familiar Spitfire, and the decision was taken to promote it as a completely new aircraft. At first it was to be called The Victor. Then, for some unaccountable reason, Vickers decided to call it the Spiteful instead.

The new aircraft went into production as the Supermarine Spiteful XIV (carrying on the Spitfire numbering system), and the Air Ministry placed an initial order for 150 planes. No sooner had the order been placed than the Ministry had an abrupt change of heart. By 1945, jet fighters were clearly the way forward and the Spiteful seemed obsolete.

✛ L-R: Jeffrey Quill; The third Royal Air Force Supermarine Spiteful FXIV FRONT VIEW; The third Royal Air Force Supermarine Spiteful FXIV SIDE VIEW TOP: Supermarine Spiteful line drawing

Supermarine Seafang ✛

The order was abruptly cancelled, with less than twenty Spitefuls ever coming off the production line. None ever entered RAF service. The Royal Navy then showed some interest, based on fears that jets would never be able to operate from aircraft carriers. A naval version was then produced called the Seafang, but when jet tests off the carrier HMS Ocean in 1945 proved successful, the Seafang was quietly just sidelined and forgotten.

Joe Smith and his team had been watching the advent of British jet technology too, and wondered if the jet engine then in development from Rolls-Royce could be combined with the Spiteful's laminar flow wing to at least salvage something from the project. The Air Ministry supported Supermarine's thinking by issuing Specification E.10/44 for a prototype 'Jet Spiteful'. The prototype, TS409, was duly built and first flown on 27 July 1946. No one was particularly impressed by it, particularly as it seemed to offer no real advantages over the Gloster Meteor or de Havilland Vampire. The RAF declined to buy it and the aircraft would have been consigned to scrap had the Admiralty not shown some interest once again. They liked the look of it and it duly entered service in a limited way with the Fleet Air Arm, now called the Attacker. 182 Attackers were produced in all.

FROM MERLIN TO GRIFFON

Rolls Royce had been working on the Griffon engine even before the war began, basing it on the R sprint engine of Schneider Trophy fame. With some ingenuity, the new engine was designed to be fitted into existing Spitfires and the first prototype Spitfire with the new Griffon engine flew in November 1941. It was essentially a converted Mk.IIA with some strengthening. The new version was initially designated the Mk.IV, then the Mk.XX before finally becoming the Mk XII in April 1942. It offered some small speed advantages over the IX below 20,000 feet but proved slower at heights greater than that.

At first it seemed that the new version did not offer any significant advantages, especially compared with the latest version of the Hawker Typhoon. Nevertheless, the RAF conducted a very simple test at Farnborough in July of 1942: They raced the Griffon-powered prototype against both the latest Hawker Typhoon and their captured Fw.190 at 2,000 feet. The Spitfire, piloted by Jeffrey Quill, won.

Anxious about Luftwaffe fighters launching low level 'tip and run' raids against targets on the south coast, the RAF initially ordered 100 MK.XIIs to meet the threat. The new Mk.XIIs were essentially Mk.Vs and Mk.VIIIs with the new Griffon engine and with their wings clipped to further enhance low level performance. The first Griffon-powered XIIs came into service with 41 Squadron in February 1943 and first shot down any enemy aircraft — a Ju.88 — over Calais on 17 April 1943. In that month 91 Squadron also received Mk.XIIs and proceeded to shoot down no less than six Fw.190 converted fighter-bombers from SKG 10 over Folkestone on the early evening of 25 May. The XII soon got a reputation amongst Luftwaffe fighter pilots, who now

showed a marked reluctance to engage with the XII at any height under 20,000 feet. One hundred were built in all.

OPERATION HUSKY

WITH NORTH AFRICA NOW FREE OF AXIS FORCES, THE ALLIES PIVOTED THEIR ATTENTION TOWARDS SICILY AND ITALY, DETERMINED TO STRIKE AT THE 'SOFT UNDERBELLY OF EUROPE.'

By June 1943, three RAF Spitfire Wings had flown north to Malta in preparation to support Operation Husky — the invasion of Sicily. Here, they typically flew as escorts for the B-24 and B-17 bomber squadrons pounding Sicily and its fortress Islands of Lampedusa and Pantelleria in preparation for invasion.

The invasion of Sicily came on the early morning of 10 July 1943, with elements of the American 7th and the British 8th Army hitting the beaches with Spitfire cover overhead. The first day saw eleven Spitfires shot down for the loss of 13 Axis aircraft. At least two of the Spitfires were brought down by friendly fire from Royal Navy warships. Both pilots were aces, and both died.

By 12 July, advancing Allied ground forces had seized the airstrip at Ponte Olivo on Sicily and the Spitfires from Malta prepared to redeploy. By the end of the next day, Luftwaffe and Regia Aeronautica resistance had weakened considerably, and Spitfires were flying in from Malta to take up residence on captured airfields. By 25 July, all enemy aircraft on Sicily had been evacuated to the mainland and those Axis ground forces still remaining started to run desperately low on supplies. They were now relying on being resupplied by Junker Ju.52 transports using the beaches at Milazzo as makeshift runways. On 25 July, thirty-three Spitfires from 322 Wing managed to slip between these transports and their Bf.109 escorts and caught them preparing to land. Many of the transports were carrying petrol and exploded in a fireball when hit. In just a few minutes, twenty-one Ju.52s were destroyed, along with four Bf.109 escorts.

With fewer and fewer Axis aircraft over Sicily, Spitfires began to participate in more ground attack missions, helping to drive the last German soldier off the island by 17 August. The next day, the Allies took Messina and all resistance on Sicily collapsed.

✈ L-R: Rolls Royce Griffon engine; Ground personnel watch as Spitfire Mark IX of No. 601 Squadron RAF, lands on the newly-completed airfield at Lentini West, Sicily; Spitfire lands at an airfield, converted from a wheat field, Sicily

THE ITALIAN CAMPAIGN

With Sicily secured, the Allies looked now to begin their invasion of Italy. On 3 September 1943, British forces streamed across the Strait of Messina to land at Reggio Calabria, under cover of a massive air umbrella. Attempts to get at both the landing forces and the shipping, often by Fw.190 fighter-bombers, was largely fought off. Within a week, all Italian forces had surrendered — but their German partners decided to fight on.

A day after Italy's surrender, American amphibious forces landed at Salerno and British forces at Taranto. Seafires and Spitfires once again flew cover in fiercely contested skies, often with 90 gallon slipper tanks to increase their time over the beachheads. By 12 September, the first Spitfires were setting up home on captured airstrips in the Salerno area.

By the autumn of 1943, Spitfire Mk.V units in Italy began to be reequipped with the Spitfire Mk.VIII, which proved exceptionally popular with the pilots. They also proved more effective against enemy Fw.190s, just at a time when Fw.190 fighter-bombers from SKG 10 were being used increasingly to hinder the Allied northwards advance. The Spitfire's role was split between providing air cover and launching ground attacks on enemy forces. Action, when it came was fast and furious as this vivid account of an action

✈ A party of riggers working on the tailplane of a Supermarine Spitfire of No. 601 Squadron at Lentini West, Sicily, 7 September 1943

over Perscara involving Lieutenant Albert 'Bertie' Sachs, SAAF, from 92 Squadron's record book for 5 December 1943 demonstrates.

'...He positioned himself behind the twelve plus fighter-bombers (Fw.190s) while two others attacked the fighter cover (Bf.109s). After destroying an Fw.190 with a one second burst, Lt Sachs saw another on the tail of a Spitfire, so he turned into it, firing a 30-degree deflection shot, then fired again from point blank range astern. The aircraft blew up and portions hit Sachs' windscreen, smashing it while another large piece struck his starboard wing.

Fw.190s were then diving on him from both sides and one shell exploded on his tailplane, blowing off his starboard elevator. He turned towards another Fw.190 which was attacking him at point blank range on his port side, and felt a jar as he collided with it. The enemy aircraft dived away out of control, minus its fin and rudder.

The attack continued and finally, after his elevator and aileron control were useless, Lt. Sachs was forced to bail out. He landed safely within his own lines within 60 yards of the wreckage of his own Spitfire.'

German air resistance began to noticeably peter out, with the Luftwaffe increasingly preferring to station what fighters they had in the north to counter bomber attacks. By November, there were estimated to be as few as 150 German fighters in the whole of Italy. With the war in the East going badly, precious German aircraft were needed more elsewhere.

By December 1943, the advancing Allies had reached the defensive Gustav line, of which Monte Cassino was an essential element. To try to outflank the Gustav Line, the Allies attempted a surprise amphibious landing behind enemy lines at Anzio to the south of Rome. With Spitfire air support, British and American troops started landing on 22 January 1944. At first things went well, but the element of surprise was not exploited. The Allies moved too cautiously, allowing German forces to launch a major counter-attack which held Allied troops in close proximity to the beaches.

By April 1944, there was by now so little threat from the air that the RAF announced that they intended to convert all Mk.VIII and Mk.IX Spitfires into fighter-bombers. An increased ground attack capability was what was needed, even if it was unpopular with most Spitfire pilots. It was inglorious — and it was dangerous. A Spitfire pilot assigned to ground attack work in Italy now had a life expectancy of just three months.

✈ L&M: Two Supermarine Spitfire Mk.IX's of 241 Squadron, flying over mountainous country south of Rome; R: Aircraftman working on the portside Merlin engine of a Spitfire on a chilly day in Southern Italy

By mid-May the Gustav Line had been breached and Allied forces streamed through to join up with the forces at Anzio. The Luftwaffe put up most of their remaining air strength to slow the Allied advance, but in doing so took unsustainable losses. Rome was captured on 4 June, by which time the Luftwaffe had started withdrawing their remaining air resources from the theatre. They were needed elsewhere to face the Allied invasion of Normandy, to fight the Soviets now racing west and, increasingly, to protect the Fatherland itself from massed Allied bombing fleets. Italy hardly mattered anymore.

✈ Some partisans are fixing a motor during a training course in a Royal Air Force aircraft base. They are doing a maintenance inspection on a Spitfire fighter-bomber. Italy, August 1944

GOODBYE FIGHTER COMMAND

In preparation for D-Day, Fighter Command was split into two. Those squadrons tasked with protecting Britain from attack were assigned to Air Defence, Great Britain, while those designated to fight in Europe became part of the 2nd Tactical Air Force. Spitfire squadrons were split between the two.

THE MK.XIV

The Spitfire Mk XIV was designed to build on the promise of the rapidly developing Griffon engine. It was essentially a Mk.VIII with a Griffon 65 engine and a two-stage supercharger, and expected to offer a considerable performance even over the much admired IX, achieving a top speed of 450 mph at 25,000 feet.

It first went into service with the RAF in January 1944 when it was supplied to 610 Squadron in Exeter. Two months later, Mk.XIVs were supplied to 91 and 322 Squadrons. Four more squadrons — 41,130,350 and 403 Squadrons — which were all part of the 2nd Tactical Air Force were reequipped with Mk.XIVs, and the XIV would go on to become the main Allied high altitude air superiority fighter in Europe until war's end.

SOFTENING UP

In the months leading up to D-Day, all the variously named unpopular RAF operations over France that had been flown since 1941 now finally seemed to have a purpose.

In preparation for D-Day itself, the Luftwaffe had to be severely reduced as a threat in the air and the Wehrmacht needed to be taken apart as an effective fighting force on the ground.

From the start of 1944, a variety of Spitfire types were used for both bombing and strafing ground targets including tanks and vehicle columns, troop concentrations and — in particular — the trains, depots and stations on France's railway network. In the last six weeks before D-Day it was estimated that 1,500 of the 2,000 railway engines of Region Nord were successfully knocked out. Closer to the coast, Spitfires and typhoons blitzed German radar stations on an almost daily basis. By the eve of D-Day, just one was working. Between Brittany and Calais 152 Spitfires were lost or damaged in the first six months of 1944, most of them due to enemy anti-aircraft fire. The Luftwaffe succeeded in downing just 21 Spitfires.

Spitfire photoreconnaissance aircraft flew daring low level missions over just about every French beach on the Channel coast, both to bring back vital information and to keep the Germans guessing as to where the invasion would come.

 L-R: Four Spitfire F Mark XIVs, flying in loose starboard echelon formation over South-east England; Refueling Spitfire XIV; Spitfire Mk XIV flown by the CO of No. 610 Squadron RAF, Squadron Leader R A Newbury, based at Friston, Sussex, 3 July 1944

D-DAY AND BEYOND

Fifty five Squadrons of Spitfires were assigned to provide air cover for the Normandy Landings on 6 June 1944 and each got a new paint scheme for the occasion. Prominent black and white stripes were added to both their wings and fuselages to aid with aircraft identification. The main role of the Spitfires was to fly low cover, while the P-47 Thunderbolts flew high cover.

In the event, very few Luftwaffe aircraft made an appearance over the invasion beaches that day. In contrast the Allies flew almost 15,000 sorties and as one Spitfire pilot commented, the greatest danger was colliding with another friendly plane in skies jam-packed with friendly aircraft.

Spitfire pilot Arthur Bradford, on a reconnaissance mission over the beaches, did get shot down by coastal flak batteries. He ended up in the Channel and was pulled on board one of the landing craft as it headed for the beaches. As the ramp came down, he too was forced to storm ashore armed only with a water-drenched service pistol. He recalled later, *'I headed for a concrete wall and hid behind it for three days!'*

The Luftwaffe rallied and attacked the beaches during daylight on 7 June, but were beaten off with heavy losses. Canadian Spitfire units alone claimed thirteen kills on that day. Within a few days, the Allies set up makeshift airstrips in France and RAF Spitfire squadrons flew the Channel to take up residence there. Some Spitfires — jokingly designated Spitfire Mk.XXXs — flew in with 18 gallon beer barrels fitted to their special bomb racks as a treat for the troops.

Now based in France, they could range still further and wider, launching attacks behind German lines on anything that

moved. On 17 July, a Spitfire from 602 Squadron shot up a German staff car in which Field Marshall Rommel was riding, seriously wounding him. In late August 1944, a retreating Wehrmacht found themselves trapped in a pocket around Falaise and were utterly pulverised from the air by rocket-firing Typhoons and Spitfire fighter-bombers. Hundreds of German tanks and vehicles were destroyed, and an estimated 10,000 enemy troops killed. By the start of September 1944, the Luftwaffe had begun to pull back to Germany to re-equip and train new pilots and there was little opposition to the Allies in the Air. As the Allies moved forward, so did the air bases, allowing Spitfires to provide both an increasingly effective air umbrella and offering close air support to the troops as they advanced. The Spitfire Squadrons of 2TAF now enjoyed air bases in Belgium and Holland.

WING TO WING

On 13 June 1944, the first three V-1 pilotless flying bombs fell on England. Six people were killed. Twenty-six foot long and packed with 1,870lb of high explosives, the V-1 was a relative crude device. It was fired from launch ramps along the French and Dutch coasts towards England and was powered by a pulse-jet engine with a range of 150 miles and at a speed of up to 400 mph. When the fuel ran out, after typically 25 minutes, it fell out of the sky — and detonated. The attack did not come as a surprise. Bomber Command had already hit the rocket research and manufacturing plant at Peenemunde the previous year, and Spitfires and Hurricanes had been launching ground attacks against the coastal launch sites since January 1944. It had not been enough to stop what Hitler called his Vergeltungswaffen or 'Vengeance Weapons'.

✈ Spitfire PR Mark XI, of 541 Squadron RAF

✈ L-R: 345th Fighter Squadron — P-47 Thunderbolts; RAF men work on a damaged Supermarine Spitfire Mk IX of 403 Squadron, Royal Canadian Air Force, at a forward airstrip in Normandy, 19 June 1944; Australian pilots of No 453 Squadron help to flatten the airstrip at Longues-sur-Mer

and Mosquitos among them. Their missions were called 'Diver Patrols'. Initially, the Spitfires of 1 and 165 Squadrons were assigned to the task but their IXs and XIIs struggled to catch the flying bombs and the XIVs of 91, 322 and 610 Squadrons were brought in to do the job. The new Gloster Meteor jet was also sent into action, but problems with its cannon meant that it only ever shot down thirteen V-1s.

Destroying the V-1s from the air proved to be challenging. Machine guns tended to have little effect on its sheet metal construction, while accurate cannon fire would cause the V-1 to explode in mid-air, almost certainly destroying the pursuing fighter at any range under 150 yards in a fireball of burning fuel and a shower of lethal metal fragments. Incredibly, some fighter pilots tried a different method. They would hare after the V-1, then touch wings, knocking the rocket bomb off kilter and sending it plummeting to the ground. This tactic, however, almost invariably resulted in some damage to the fighter's wing tip. In just a very short space of time, pilots worked out that if they could position their wing at an optimum distance of six inches under the V-1s wing, the airflow moving over the fighter's wing would force the V-1's wing up. The inbuilt gyroscope on the rocket bomb would not be able to compensate and the V-1 would tip over and crash. It was a mad — and quite incredible feat of flying.

On 15 June, 55 Nazi rocket sites unleashed a barrage of 244 V-1s. Seventy three of them fell in the Greater London area. Three days later, a torrent of 500 V-1s were unleashed against London. In just one month, 2,754 rained down on Southern England and London.

By July 1944, London's anti-aircraft guns had multiplied and the airspace over London was bristling with barrage balloons. On the south coast, incoming V-1s were having to run a gauntlet of 1,600 AA guns, and air controllers had moved into local Royal Observer Corps posts to alert fighter aircraft to incoming V-1s and to guide them to their target.

A wide variety of fast Allied aircraft were used to try and chase and destroy the V-1s over the Channel or in the airspace between the coastal guns and the capital itself at typical heights of 3-4,000 feet — Tempests, P-47s, P-51s

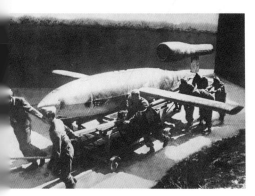

✚ L-R: V1 is rolled to the launcher; Twin 5.25-inch guns of an anti-aircraft battery at Primrose Hill in London; This V-1 made it through air defenses and fell on London TOP: V-1_cutaway diagram

✚ L-R: Metz Airfield — Destroyed P-47s during Operation Bodenplatte

Almost 2,500 civilians were killed by V-1s and another 35,000 injured, but by the beginning of September 1944, the threat was almost over, thanks to the launch sites either being bombed into oblivion or overrun by Allied troops. ADGB fighters in total accounted for 1,846 V-1s, 303 of which were brought down by Spitfires. Anti-aircraft guns and barrage balloons claimed another 2,109.

That same month, just as the V-1 menace diminished, the Germans unleashed the V-2, a rocket with a one ton explosive payload. The V-2 was fired into the air and after reaching an altitude of some fifty miles, it would simply run out of fuel and drop back to earth on its target at supersonic speed. There was no hope whatsoever of any aircraft intercepting these. Instead, the RAF went after their launch sites in Holland with Spitfires, dive-bombing the sites with either a single 500lb bomb or two 250 lbs bombs. The Spitfire raids met with a degree of success but only the Allied ground offensive through the Netherlands truly stopped the V-2 threat.

BODENPLATTE

On New Year's Day 1945, the Luftwaffe made one last desperate attempt to gain a measure of aerial superiority in Europe with Operation Bodenplatte. Massed German formations of some 800 fighters launched a surprise attack on Allied airfields, hoping to have a devastating effect on Allied aircraft numbers. It failed, not least because many of the Luftwaffe pilots were comparative novices and had only received a poor, rushed standard of training. Spitfires shot down at least thirty-two German fighters over the course

of the day. Thirteen Spitfires were lost — seven in actual dogfights while the rest were destroyed on the ground. The Luftwaffe never recovered, losing 270 fighters and 143 badly needed pilots in the raids. There were just seventeen weeks of the war left to fight and the Luftwaffe now had next to nothing to fly in opposition. Increasingly, Spitfires flew unchallenged over a burning and devastated Reich.

THE MARK 21

'The beautiful symmetry had gone; in its place stood a powerful, almost ugly fighting machine'
Alex Henshaw on the Mk 21

The Spitfire Mark 21 was not received well. Test pilots from the Air Fighting Development Unit conducted trials in December 1944 and found it both difficult and uncomfortable to fly, with serious rudder problems in particular. Their scathing report concluded, *'No further attempts should be made to perpetuate the Spitfire family.'*

Jeffrey Quill regarded the 21 as a *'hot potato'* from the first time he test flew it. *'There was too much power and too much performance,'* he said.

In reality, the rudder problems were solved quite quickly when both rudder and tail were increased in size, and the Mk.21 went on to prove itself. However, the damage was done and an official order for 3,000 Mk.21s placed in May 1945 was cut to just 120 aircraft. By then the war was won.

✈ Two Pilots of the Australian Spitfire Squadron wish a colleague
"good hunting" before his take off

JL244 7

✈ Two pilots observing a British Spitfire fighter jet formation flying
over a 12th Allied Air Force base. France, October 1944

PASSING INTO LEGEND

POST WAR SERVICE

BY THE TIME WORLD WAR TWO WAS OVER, THE RAF
HAD NO LESS THAN 5,864 SPITFIRES IN ITS POSSESSION
– AND NO-ONE TO FIGHT.

Within less than a year, Fighter Command had whittled
its Spitfire squadrons down to just two — 41 and 63
Squadrons. The volunteer Royal Auxiliary Air Force though
flew Spitfires in thirteen of its twenty squadrons and —
when that fell under the control of Fighter Command in
1949 — technically there were still fifteen Spitfire squadrons
still flying. Until 1948, new marks of Spitfires were still being
bought and pressed into service. The Mk.22 saw a brief
time in service with an RAF Squadron before being handed
over to the Royal Auxiliary Air Force.

The very last Spitfire Mark was the Mk.24, which was first
flown on 13 April 1946. Just eighty-one were produced
(twenty-seven of which were converted from Mk.22s). Mark
24s were supplied to 80 Squadron serving in Occupied
Germany to replace their Hawker Tempests. In 1949, 80
Squadron left for its new home at Kai-Tak in Hong Kong.
The last RAF Spitfires based in occupied Japan — the
Mk.XIV's of 17 Squadron — left in the spring of 1948.

The final Spitfire came off the production line at the Vickers
Supermarine Works at South Marston, near Swindon, in
the spring of 1948. This was designated VN496. On 4 April
1948, the day it was due to be supplied to the RAF, deputy
chief test pilot Squadron Leader Guy Morgan took VN496
up and flew it over the grave of R.J. Mitchell in South
Stoneham Cemetery. VN496 is now on display with the
Imperial War Museum at Duxford.

Spitfires were still fighting with the RAF though. In 1948,
two squadrons of Spitfires based in Singapore were used to
combat guerrilla insurgents during the Malayan Emergency,
and fought there for three years mostly in a ground attack
role, strafing, bombing and rocketing Communist positions
and troop concentrations in the jungle. The final combat
mission by Spitfires was flown on 1 January 1951, by which
time Spitfires had flown approximately 1,800 sorties. The
F.47 Seafires of 800 Squadron also played a small role in
the Malayan insurgency, flying from ground bases to launch
rocket attacks on communist jungle bases.

In June 1950, 800 Squadron Seafires also took part in the
Korean War, flying off HMS *Triumph* at first in a ground
attack role before being moved to Combat Air Patrols over

✛ TOP: MK. 22 BOTTOM: MK. 24

✛ L-R: Spitfire Mk.XVI, in flight with the white stripes of the Allied
landing in Normandy and the insignia of Air Marshal Sir James
M.Robb, Commander-in-Chief of air forces in western Europe. 1945

the fleet. *Triumph* returned to Britain in November 1950 and 800 Squadron was disbanded. This was effectively the end of the Seafire's frontline service. A total of 2,580 Seafires were built in all.

The last Spitfires in a frontline role were finally phased out in 1951 to be replaced by Meteors and Vampires, moving on to a role with the Anti-Aircraft Co-Operation Units until they too were finally done away with in 1954. The very final official Spitfire flight was made on 21 April 1955 in Hong Kong, where Mk.24 Spitfires performed a fly-past to salute the Queen's birthday.

THE GREAT SPITFIRE SALE

Even as the Spitfire continued on a limited role in the immediate post-war RAF, there were still over five and a half thousand Spitfires that were superfluous to requirement and which the government were keen to get off the books. Most went, unsentimentally, to scrapyards, but others were sold abroad.

The Egyptian Air Force acquired thirty-seven Mk.IX's in 1946, Thailand bought thirty Mk.IVs in 1948, and Belgium purchased 132 Mk.IV's in a three year period from 1948 to

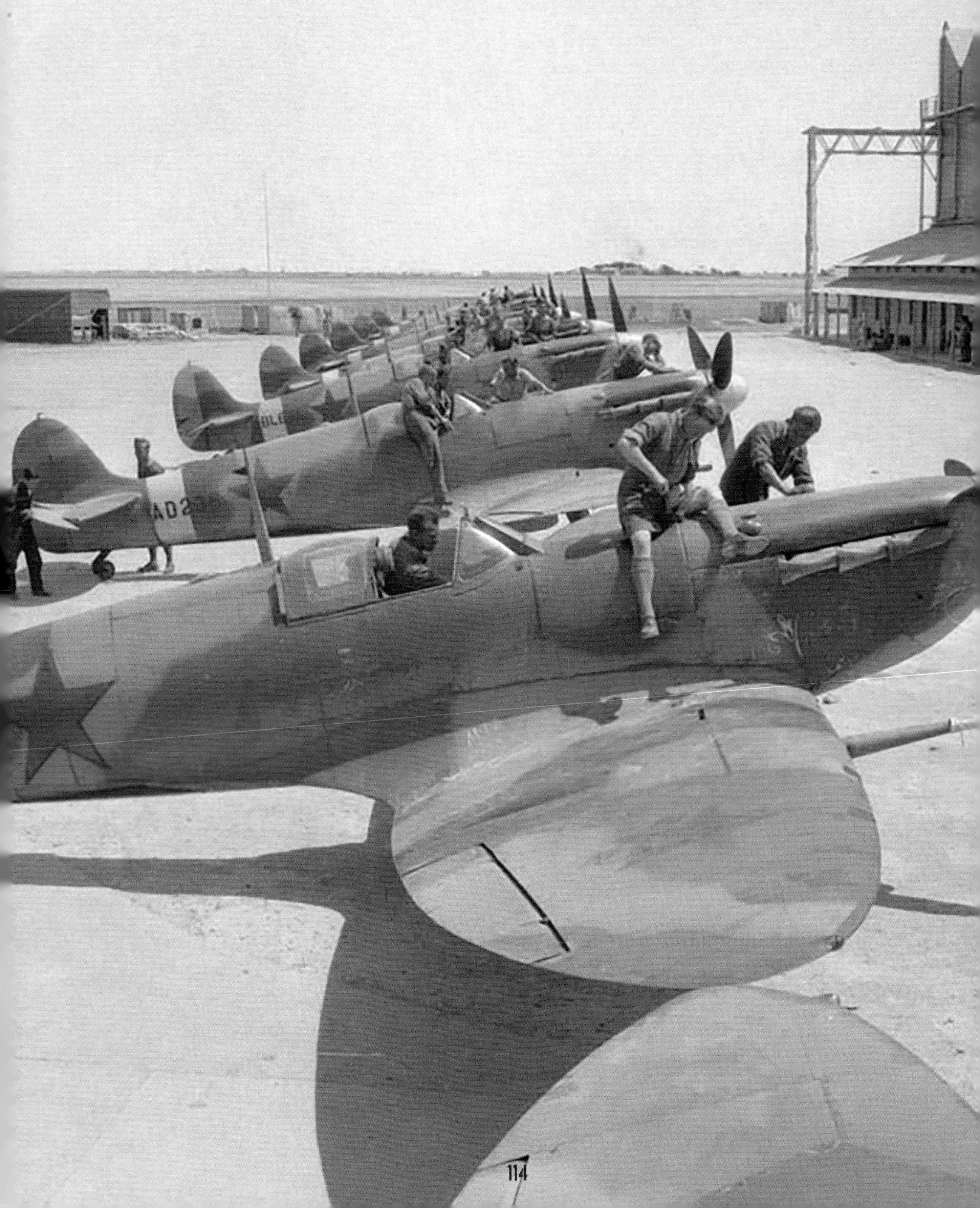

1950. The Swedish Air Force picked up fifty XIX's brand new in 1950 to replace their old Junkers 86Ks. Burma picked up three Mk.VIIIS to fly beside their Seafires in the fight against communist guerrillas. These were not the only Air Forces eager to possess Spitfires in the immediate post-war world. Spitfires also flew in the air forces of Denmark, Greece, India, Italy, the Netherlands, Norway, Portugal, South Africa, Southern Rhodesia, Syria, Turkey and Yugoslavia. In total over fifty air forces around the globe flew Spitfires post-war.

The Soviet Union, never great fans of the Spitfire, took the opportunity to sell some of their surplus Spitfire Mk.IX's to the Communist Chinese — but what actually happened to these aircraft remains a matter of mystery.

Czech RAF pilots proudly returned home with their Spitfires after the war, only to have their nation seized by Communists in a coup. Following the coup, Czechoslovakia sold a number of these Spitfires on to the fledgling Israeli Air Force. During the 1948 War of Independence, this led to the unique spectacle of Spitfires dogfighting with other Spitfires as the IAF clashed with the Royal Egyptian Air Force. To complicate matters further, the RAF still had Spitfire squadrons in the area and a number were shot

✈ L-R: Egyptian Air force; Spitfire in service with the Royal Netherlands Air Force; Spitfire in service with the Norweigan air force TOP RIGHT: Belgian air force

✈ Spitfires being checked before delivery to Russia

down or destroyed on the ground in the confusion, with both sides mistaking them for enemy aircraft.

SPITFIRES IN PRESERVATION

20,351 Spitfires and Seafires were built in all. Today, a little over fifty are still flying around the world — twenty-two of which assembled together at Duxford in 2000 to mark the 60th anniversary of the Battle of Britain. Perhaps as many as seventy survive as static displays on airfields and in museums and a further 110 are estimated to be in storage or preservation. The earliest surviving Spitfire — the 155th to be built — can be seen at RAF Cosford. There are ersatz replicas and kits too, some of which commit the cardinal sin of having a Japanese engine.

At a time when Spitfires by the thousands were lying on scrapheaps, being sold off to minor league air forces around the world or being gutted to stand as 'gate guardians', it began to be understood that the Spitfire was something

truly special and worthy of preservation. What the people of Britain had grasped and appreciated in that perilous summer of 1940 had been largely forgotten by 1945, certainly by politicians. The Spitfire had turned from a miraculous saviour into just a war machine — a quite marvellous one to be sure, but still something less than a legend.

Now some began to remember again, and to want to mark the achievements of the Spitfire and to celebrate what it meant. The RAF Historic Aircraft flight was formed at Biggin Hill in 1957 to keep the spitfire flying. It begged, stole or borrowed more Spitfires both to fly and to cannibalise for spare parts. Today, its legacy is the RAF's Battle of Britain Memorial Flight, which has possession of six Spitfires. It makes dozens of appearances at UK air shows every year and is one of the star attractions.

The public kept the Spitfire alive in its heart too. Spitfire pilot memoirs were best-sellers in the decade after the war, and many were made into feature films. Every boy raised in

✢ Spitfire and Hawker Hurricane flying parallel in the sky at the annual Scotlands National Airshow in East Fortune

the 1960s would instantly know and love the Spitfire from reading about their exploits in The Victor comic, the Air Ace Picture Library or the adventures of Biggles. They would construct Airfix Spitfire kits (price Two Shillings) and hang them from strings off their bedroom ceilings.

While every boy could own a model kit, owning the real thing is undoubtedly a rich man's preserve, and flying Spitfires have soared in value in recent years. In 2015, a fully restored ex-92 Squadron Mk.I Spitfire sold for £3.1 million at a Christie's auction. It had been rescued from its crash site on a French beach, after being shot down by a D0.217 bomber over Dunkirk in 1940. The previous record for a Spitfire was £1,739,500 for a two seater trainer version of the Mk.IX in 2009. It should be noted that the costs of maintaining and flying a Spitfire are equally stratospheric. Fuel alone accounts for £500 for each hour of flying time.

For those whose means do not stretch to owning a Spitfire, there are a handful of companies offering flights in two

seater Spitfires. Lucky guests can fly close to the White Cliffs of Dover or even — constitution permitting — engage in some aerobatics. Unsurprisingly, the price for such an experience may be several thousand pounds.

Spitfires are in increasing demand to fly over everything from lavish classical music and fireworks events at grand stately homes to country fetes — and no commemorative or celebratory flypast in the nation is ever truly complete without the Spitfire gracing it.

Today, though, it's the Air Show where most people still experience the Spitfire in all its grace and glory, accompanied by the distinctive sound of the Merlin or Griffon, and where people of an older generation still try to explain to ice-cream devouring little children how very much the Spitfire means to Britain.

THE SPITFIRE ACES

ADOLPH 'SAILOR' MALAN

27 KILLS   7 SHARED   3 PROBABLES

'Sailor Malan was the best pilot of the war; a good tactician, an above average pilot and an excellent shot.'
Air Commodore Alan Deere

A South African who joined the RAF in 1936, Malan achieved five kills over Dunkirk in 1940 and went on to command the Spitfires of 74 Squadron during the Battle of Britain. Malan wrote a 'Tips List' for other fighter pilots which was shared far and wide throughout Fighter Command:

TEN OF MY RULES FOR AIR FIGHTING

1. Wait until you see the whites of his eyes. Fire short bursts of one to two seconds only when your sights are definitely "ON".

2. Whilst shooting think of nothing else, brace the whole of your body: have both hands on the stick: concentrate on your ring sight.

3. Always keep a sharp lookout. "Keep your finger out".

4. Height gives you the initiative.

5. Always turn and face the attack.

6. Make your decisions promptly. It is better to act quickly even though your tactics are not the best.

7. Never fly straight and level for more than 30 seconds in the combat area.

8. When diving to attack always leave a proportion of your formation above to act as a top guard.

9. Initiative, aggression, air discipline, and teamwork are words that mean something in Air Fighting.

10. Go in quickly — Punch hard — Get out!

Malan survived the war and returned to South Africa where he became a fierce opponent of apartheid.

JAMES 'JOHNNIE' JOHNSON

34 KILLS   7 SHARED   3 SHARED PROBABLES

A native of Melton Mowbray in Leicestershire, Johnson initially applied to join the Auxiliary Air Force in the 1930s, but was turned down because his father was a mere police constable and he was not a member of either of Melton's celebrated Hunts. It was only when social barriers were lifted somewhat that Johnson was permitted to join the Royal Air Force Volunteer Reserve in 1939 and go on to become both the top Allied western fighter ace against the Luftwaffe and an Air Vice Marshal.

Johnson missed virtually all of the Battle of Britain due to a reoccurring injury. By 1941, he was heavily involved in the sector offensive sweeps over Europe — which he hated. Unusually, Johnson's confirmed kills were all German fighters — 14 Bf.109s and 20 Fw.190s.

Johnson survived the war — and the Korean War in which he also fought.

BRENDAN 'PADDY' FINUCANE

28 KILLS   6 SHARED   5 PROBABLES

An Irish Catholic whose family moved to England in 1936, Finucane joined the RAF in 1938 and gained his wings only after some difficulties in 1939. Finucane scored two kills and two 'probables' during the Battle of Britain while flying Spitfires. With his youthful good looks and prominent Shamrock motif on his Spitfire, he became something of a 'pin-up boy' during the Battle, publicized by the RAF and bombarded by fan mail (and marriage proposals) from young female fans. The Chicago Herald referred to him as the 'Flying Shamrock terror of the Nazis.'

By April 1941 he was flying offensive fighter sweeps over Europe and notching up significant kills, mostly against German fighter aircraft. In June 1942, he became the RAF'S youngest-ever Wing Commander when he took command of the Hornchurch Wing at the age of 21. Barely a month later, on 15 July 1942, his Spitfire was hit by anti-aircraft fire and crashed in the Channel. Finucane was killed.

DOUGLAS BADER

22 KILLS   4 SHARED   6 PROBABLES

'He was always, always looking for a fight.'
Hugh Dundas

Douglas Bader is today perhaps the most famous of the Spitfire Aces. A Londoner from a relatively wealthy family, Bader joined the RAF in 1928. In 1931, while performing low level aerobatics on a dare, he crashed his Bristol Bulldog and lost both of his legs. His log book for the day merely reads 'Crashed slow-rolling near ground. Bad show.'

Incredibly, after convalescing he was permitted to fly again, having been fitted with artificial 'tin' legs. Bader's first kill, a Bf.109, was over Dunkirk. He went on to score a number of kills during the Battle of Britain flying Hurricanes. He also became a vocal critic of Dowding's tactics and a fierce advocate of the 'Big Wing' approach favoured by Leigh-Mallory. 1941 saw him promoted to Wing Commander and flying Spitfires on offensive sweeps over Europe with the radio call sign 'Dogsbody'. During this time, his kills were mainly BF.109s. On 9 August 1941, he was brought down under somewhat confused circumstances over France and captured. He spent the rest of the war in a POW camp, participating in his favourite sport of 'goon-baiting' and generally making life as miserable as he could for his guards. He also participated in so many escape attempts that, in exasperation, the Germans threatened to take away his artificial legs if he didn't behave.

After the war, Bader visited a Luftwaffe pilot's reunion in Munich as the special guest of Adolf Galland. He looked around the room where the veterans were gathered and then said, *'My God! — I had no idea we left so many of you bastards alive...'*

ALAN 'AL' DEERE

22 KILLS   10 PROBABLES

A New Zealander, 'Al' Deere went from flying Gloster Gladiators to Spitfires in 1940. He described his Spitfire as 'the most beautiful and easy aircraft to fly.' He claimed his first kills over Northern France in 1940, claiming three Bf.109s in a single day. He was shot down by a Dorner 217 gunner over Dunkirk and only returned to England after waiting his turn to be evacuated off the beaches. He was back in the air in less than a day.

Deere fought through the Battle of Britain, accounting for eight enemy aircraft between July and September 1944. By 1942, he was a Wing Leader at Biggin Hill, adding four more kills to his tally. By 1944, he was commander of the Free French Fighter Wing, leading them out over the beaches of Normandy on 6 June.

Deere survived the war and ended up as the Director of RAF Rugby (the sport, not the town). When he died in 1995, his ashes were scattered on the River Thames by a Spitfire.

ROBERT STANFORD TUCK

27 KILLS   2 SHARED KILLS   6 PROBABLES

Born in London to Jewish parents, Tuck was one of the RAF's first Spitfire aces, bringing down seven enemy aircraft over Dunkirk. He alternated between Spitfires and Hurricanes during the Battle of Britain, with his score rising to fourteen enemy aircraft while on Spitfires.

In December 1941, Tuck was appointed commander of the Biggin Hill Wing. The following January he was shot down over France by anti-aircraft fire while on a low-level 'Rhubarb' mission and was taken prisoner. He escaped on 1 February 1945 and spent some time fighting alongside the Soviet Red Army before being shipped back to Britain. Tuck took part in the interrogation of captured German ace Adolf Galland but admitted, 'mostly we just fed him cigars and wine and, you know, just talked…' After leaving the RAF, Tuck became a test pilot and then a mushroom farmer.

NEVILLE DUKE

27 KILLS 2 PROBABLES

Neville Duke was the top Allied air ace in the Mediterranean theatre during World War Two. His first two kills came flying Spitfires over occupied Europe in 1941 before he was transferred to North Africa. Here he scored another eight kills flying the P-40 Tomahawk before returning to the Spitfire Mk.V. Happier flying the Spitfire, he brought down another 14 Axis aircraft as part of 92 Squadron. Five more kills were to follow, flying the Spitfire Mk.VIII over Italy. In June 1944, while on a ground strafing mission he was shot down by anti-aircraft fire, but evaded capture with the help of local partisans.

Duke survived the war and, ironically, went on to become Hawker's chief test pilot. He broke the World Air Speed record in 1953.

ERIC 'SAWN OFF LOCKIE' LOCK

26 KILLS   1 SHARED KILL   8 PROBABLES

Eric Lock was very short, which resulted in his nickname of 'Sawn Off'. This did not stop him marrying a former 'Miss Shrewsbury' in July 1940. Despite not flying his first operational sortie until 9 August 1940, Eric Lock became the second most successful RAF pilot during the Battle of Britain, accounting for 21 Luftwaffe aircraft. He scored another five kills on operational sweeps over occupied France during the early months of 1941.

On 3 August 1941, Lock was returning from a 'Rhubarb' over France when he spotted a troop convoy. He broke away from his formation and went to strafe the vehicles. Lock was never seen again. It is believed he was hit by anti-aircraft fire and crashed in the Channel.

138

GEORGE 'SCREWBALL' BEURLING   31 KILLS

'...he was a wonderful pilot and an even better shot.'
Ginger Lacey

George Beurling was a Canadian national who made
his formidable reputation in the skies over Malta in 1942
where it is said he shot down 27 Axis aircraft in just a single
fortnight.

Beurling's lack of academic qualifications led to him being
turned down by the Royal Canadian Air Force, so he sailed
to England to join the RAF. Unfortunately, he had forgotten
to pack his birth certificate. He had to sail all the way back
to Canada again to get it, and on his return was finally
accepted by the RAF in September 1940.

Beurling ended up in Malta by accident. He had swapped
places with another pilot and had no idea where he would
end up. Intensely self-disciplined — but a crazy flier who
would push his Spitfire beyond all the accepted limits
— Beurling became an ace in just a four day period and
went on to score the vast majority of his kills over Malta.
Wounded in a dogfight in October 1942, he was evacuated
back to England and 'rested'. In 1943, he joined the RCAF
and flew Spitfire IX's before the disciplinary problems that
had plagued his flying career saw him moved around and
finally discharged in October 1944.

Beurling survived the war, but could not adapt to peacetime.
He died in 1948 in Rome, accidentally crashing his
transport aircraft on the way to join the Israeli Air Force.

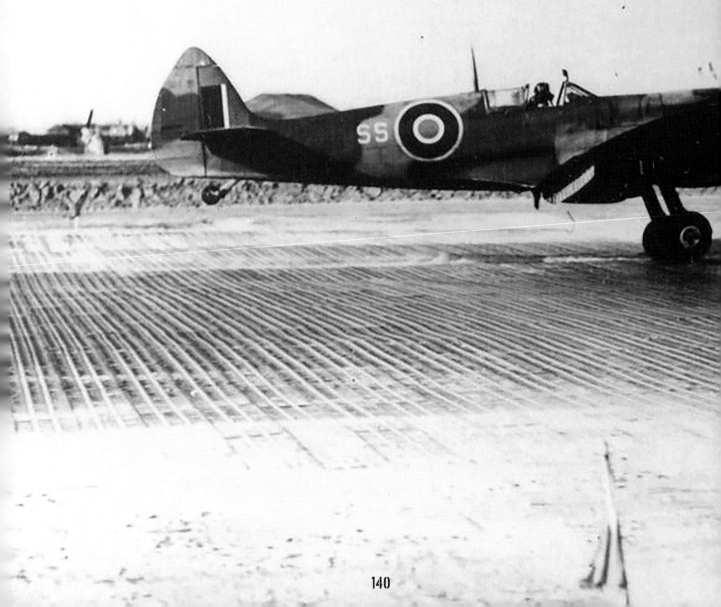

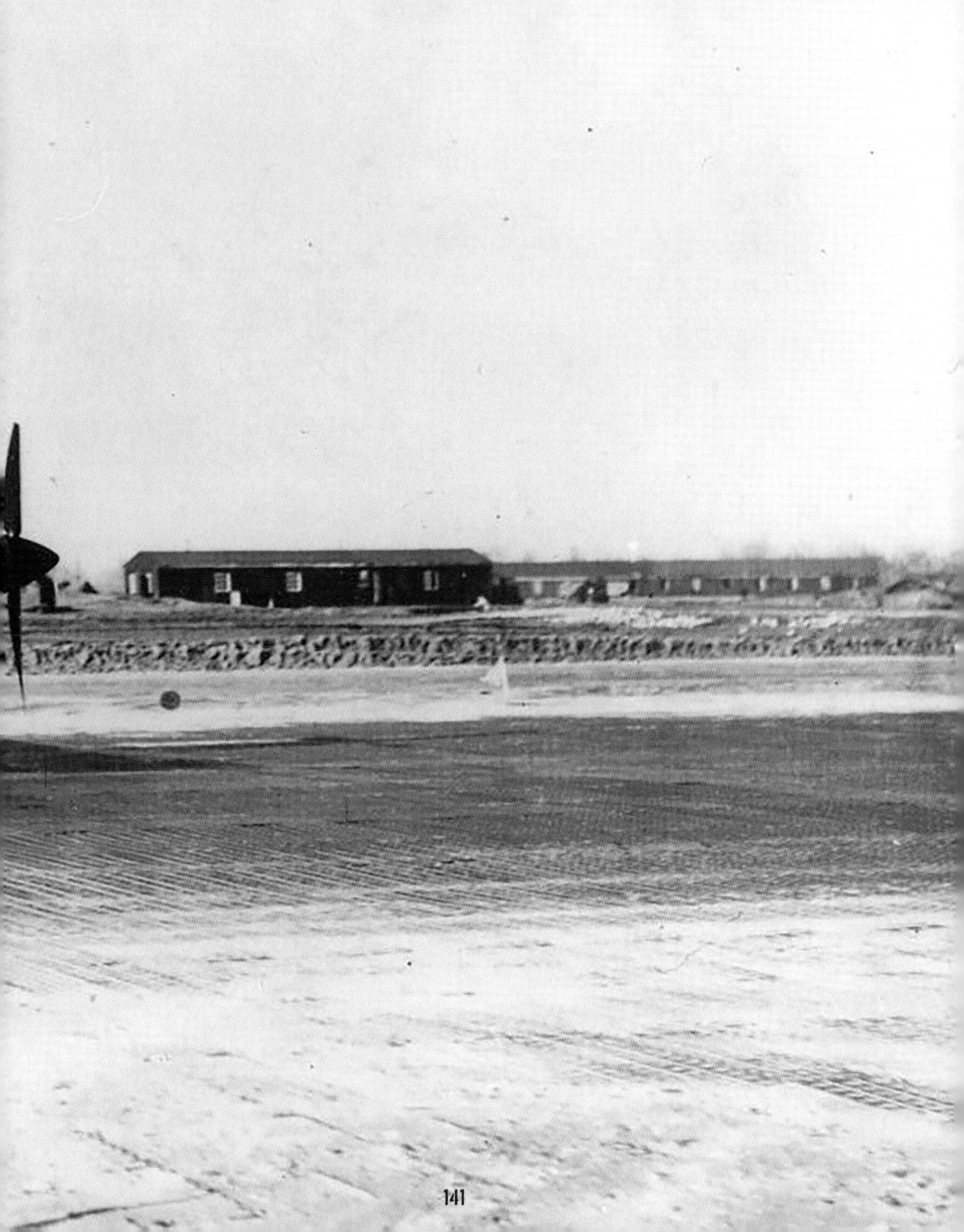